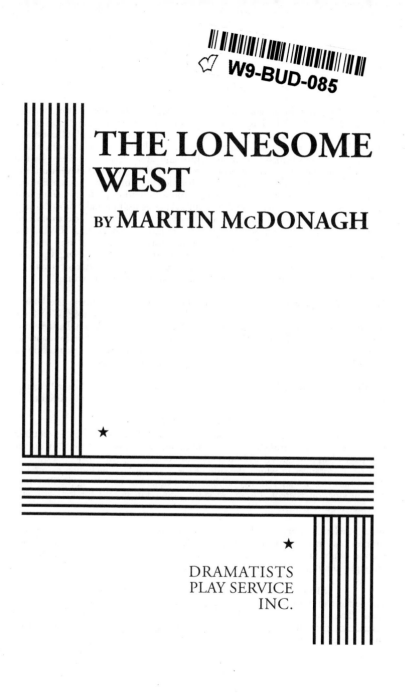

THE LONESOME WEST

BY MARTIN McDONAGH

DRAMATISTS
PLAY SERVICE
INC.

THE LONESOME WEST
Copyright © 1997, 1999, Martin McDonagh

All Rights Reserved

SPECIAL NOTE

SPECIAL NOTE ON SONGS AND RECORDINGS

THE LONESOME WEST was produced by Druid Theatre
Company/Royal Court Theatre, at Town Hall Theatre, Galway,
Ireland, on June 10, 1997. The production subsequently opened
at the Royal Court Theatre Downstairs, in London, as part of
THE LEENANE TRILOGY, on July 19, 1997. It was directed by
Garry Hynes; the set design was by Francis O'Connor; the
lighting design was by Ben Ormerod; the sound design was by
Bell Helicopter; the original music was by Paddy Cunneen; and
the production managers were Maurice Power (Druid) and Ed
Wilson (RCT). The cast was as follows:

GIRLEEN KELLEHER . . . . Dawn Bradfield
FATHER WELSH . . . . David Ganly
COLEMAN CONNOR . . . . Maelíosa Stafford
VALENE CONNOR . . . . Brían F. O'Byrne

CHARACTERS

GIRLEEN KELLEHER — 17
FATHER WELSH — Late 20s, early 30s
COLEMAN CONNOR — 40s
VALENE CONNOR— 40s

THE LONESOME WEST

ACT ONE

Scene 1

The kitchen/living-room of an old farmhouse in Leenane, Galway. Front door far right, table with two chairs down right, an old fireplace in the center of the back wall, tattered armchairs to its right and left. Door to Coleman's room in the left back wall. Door to Valene's room far left. A long row of dusty, plastic Catholic figurines, each marked with a black 'V', line a shelf on the back wall, above which hangs a double-barrelled shotgun and above that a large crucifix. A food cupboard on the wall left, a chest of drawers towards the right, upon which rests a framed photo of a black dog. As the play begins it is day. Coleman, dressed in black, having just attended a funeral, enters, undoing his tie. He takes a biscuit tin out of a cupboard, tears off the Sellotape that binds its lid and takes out from it a bottle of poteen, also marked with a 'V'. Father Welsh, a young priest, enters just behind him.

WELSH.   I'll leave the door for Valene.
COLEMAN.   Be doing what you like. *(He pours two glasses as Welsh sits at the table.)* You'll have a drink with me you will?
WELSH.   I will, Coleman, so.
COLEMAN.   *(Quietly.)* A dumb fecking question that was.
WELSH.   Eh?

COLEMAN.   I said a dumb fecking question that was.

WELSH.   Why, now? *(Coleman gives Welsh his drink without answering and sits at the table also.)* Don't be swearing today of all days anyway, Coleman.

COLEMAN.   I'll be swearing if I want to be swearing.

WELSH.   After us only burying your dad, I'm saying.

COLEMAN.   Oh aye, right enough, sure you know best, oh aye.

WELSH.   *(Pause.)* Not a bad turnout anyways.

COLEMAN.   A pack of vultures only coming nosing.

WELSH.   Come on now, Coleman. They came to pay their last respects.

COLEMAN.   Did seven of them, so, not come up asking where the booze-up after was to be held, and Maryjohnny then 'Will ye be having vol-au-vents?' There'll be no vol-au-vents had in this house for the likes of them. Not while Valene holds the purse-strings anyways. If it was me held the purse-strings I'd say aye, come around for yourselves, even if ye are vultures, but I don't hold the purse-strings. Valene holds the purse-strings.

WELSH.   Valene does be a biteen tight with his money.

COLEMAN.   A biteen? He'd steal the shite out of a burning pig, and this is his poteen too, so if he comes in shouting the odds tell him you asked me outright for it. Say you sure enough demanded. That won't be hard to believe.

WELSH.   Like an alcoholic you paint me as half the time.

COLEMAN.   Well that isn't a big job of painting. A bent child with no paint could paint you as an alcoholic. There's no great effort needed in that.

WELSH.   I never touched the stuff before I came to this parish. This parish would drive you to drink.

COLEMAN.   I suppose it would, only some people don't need as much of a drive as others. Some need only a short walk.

WELSH.   I'm no alcoholic, Coleman. I like to drink is all.

COLEMAN.   Oh aye, and I believe you too. *(Pause.)* Vol-au-vents, feck. The white-haired oul ghoulish fecking whore. She's owed me the price of a pint since nineteen-seventy-fecking-seven. It's always tomorrow with that bitch. I don't care if she does have Alzheimer's. If I had a vol-au-vent I'd shove it up her arse.

6

WELSH. That's not a nice thing to be saying about a....

COLEMAN. I don't care if it is or it isn't.

WELSH. *(Pause.)* This house, isn't it going to be awful lonesome now with yere dad gone?

COLEMAN. No.

WELSH. Ah it'll be a biteen lonesome I'm sure.

COLEMAN. If you're saying it'll be a biteen lonesome maybe it *will* be a biteen lonesome. I'll believe it if you're forcing it down me throat and sure aren't you the world's authority on lonesome?

WELSH. Are there no lasses on the horizon for ye, now ye're free and easy? Oh I'll bet there's hundreds.

COLEMAN. Only your mammy.

WELSH. It's a beautiful mood today you're in. *(Pause.)* Were you never in love with a girl, so, Coleman?

COLEMAN. I was in love with a girl one time, aye, not that it's any of your fecking business. At tech this was. Alison O'Hoolihan. This gorgeous red hair on her. But she got a pencil stuck in the back of her gob one day. She was sucking it the pointy-end inwards. She must've gotten a nudge. That was the end of me and Alison O'Hoolihan.

WELSH. Did she die, Coleman?

COLEMAN. She didn't die, no. I wish she had, the bitch. No, she got engaged to the bastarding doctor who wrenched the pencil out for her. Anybody could've done that job. It didn't need a doctor. I have no luck. *(Pause. Welsh drinks some more. Valene enters with a carrier bag out of which he takes some new figurines and arranges them on the shelf. Coleman watches.)*

VALENE. Fibreglass.

COLEMAN. *(Pause.)* Feck fibreglass.

VALENE. No, feck you instead of feck fibreglass.

COLEMAN. No, feck you two times instead of feck fibreglass....

WELSH. Hey now!! *(Pause.)* Jesus!

VALENE. He started it.

WELSH. *(Pause.)* Tom Hanlon I see he's back. I was speaking to him at the funeral. Did Tom know yere dad?

COLEMAN. Slightly he knew dad. He arrested him five or six times for screaming at nuns.

WELSH. I remember hearing tell of that. That was an odd crime.

COLEMAN. Not that odd.

WELSH. Ah come on, now, it is.

COLEMAN. Oh if you say it is, Walsh, I suppose it is.

VALENE. I do hate them fecking Hanlons.

WELSH. Why now, Val?

VALENE. Why, is it? Didn't their Mairtin hack the ears off of poor Lassie, let him fecking bleed to death?

COLEMAN. You've no evidence at all it was Mairtin hacked the ears off of Lassie.

VALENE. Didn't he go bragging about it to Blind Billy Pender?

COLEMAN. That's only hearsay evidence. You wouldn't get that evidence to stand up in a court of law. Not from a blind boy anyways.

VALENE. I'd expect you to be agin me. Full well I'd expect it.

COLEMAN. That dog did nothing but bark anyways.

VALENE. Well barking doesn't deserve ears chopped off, Coleman. That's what dogs are supposed to do is bark, if you didn't know.

COLEMAN. Not at that rate of barking. They're meant to ease up now and then. That dog was going for the world's fecking barking record.

WELSH. And there's plenty enough hate in the world as it is, Valene Connor, without you adding to it over a dead dog.

VALENE. Nobody'll notice a biteen more hate, so, if there's plenty enough hate in the world.

WELSH. A nice attitude that is for a....

VALENE. Feck off and sling your sermons at Maureen Folan and Mick Dowd, so, if it's nice attitudes you're after, Walsh. Wouldn't that be more in your fecking line? *(Welsh bows his head and pours himself another drink.)*

COLEMAN. That shut the fecker up.

VALENE. It did. You see how quick he is to.... That's my fecking poteen now! What's the ... eh?

COLEMAN. He did come in pegging orders for a drink, now. What was I supposed to say to him, him just sticking dad in the ground for us?

VALENE. Your own you could've given him so.

8

COLEMAN.   And wasn't I about to 'til I up and discovered me cupboard was bare.

VALENE.   Bare again, was it?

COLEMAN.   Bare as a bald fella's arse.

VALENE.   Never unbare are your cupboards.

COLEMAN.   I suppose they're not now, but isn't that life?

WELSH.   And there's no such word as unbare. *(Valene stares at Welsh sternly.)*

COLEMAN.   *(Laughing.)* He's right!

VALENE.   Picking me up on me vocabulary is it, Welsh?

COLEMAN.   It is, aye.

WELSH.   I'm not now. I'm only codding ya, Val.

VALENE.   And shaking the hands of Mick and Maureen weren't you, too, I saw you at the grave there, and passing chit-chat among ye....

WELSH.   I was passing no chit-chat....

VALENE.   A great parish it is you run, one of them murdered his missus, an axe through her head, the other her mammy, a poker took her brains out, and it's only chit-chatting it is you be with them? Oh aye.

WELSH.   What can I do, sure, if the courts and the polis....

VALENE.   Courts and the polis me arse. I heard the fella you represent was a higher authority than the courts and the fecking polis.

WELSH.   *(Sadly.)* I heard the same thing, sure. I must've heard wrong. It seems like God has no jurisdiction in this town. No jurisdiction at all. *(Valene takes his bottle, mumbling, and pours himself a drink. Pause.)*

COLEMAN.   That's a great word, I think.

VALENE.   What word?

COLEMAN.   Jurisdiction. I like J-words.

VALENE.   Jurisdiction's too Yankee-sounding for me. They never stop saying it on *Hill Street Blues*.

COLEMAN.   It's better than unbare anyways.

VALENE.   Don't you be starting with me again, ya feck.

COLEMAN.   I will do what I wish, Mr. Figurine-man.

VALENE.   Leave me figurines out of it.

COLEMAN.   How many more do ya fecking need?

VALENE.   Lots more! No, lots and lots more!

9

COLEMAN. Oh aye.

VALENE. And where's me felt-tip pen, too, so I'll be giving them me 'V'?

COLEMAN. I don't know where your fecking felt-tip pen is.

VALENE. Well you had it doing beards in me *Woman's Own* yesterday!

COLEMAN. Aye, and you wrenched it from me near tore me hand off.

VALENE. Is all you deserved....

COLEMAN. You probably went hiding it then. *(On these words, Valene instantly remembers where his pen is and exits to his room. Pause.)* He's forever hiding things that fella.

WELSH. I'm a terrible priest, so I am. I can never be defending God when people go saying things agin him, and, sure, isn't that the main qualification for being a priest?

COLEMAN. Ah there be a lot worse priests than you, Father, I'm sure. The only thing with you is you're a bit too weedy and you're a terror for the drink and you have doubts about Catholicism. Apart from that you're a fine priest. Number one you don't go abusing poor gasurs, so, sure, doesn't that give you a head-start over half the priests in Ireland?

WELSH. That's no comfort at all, and them figures are overexaggerated anyways. I'm a terrible priest, and I run a terrible parish, and that's the end of the matter. Two murderers I have on me books, and I can't get either of the beggars to confess to it. About betting on the horses and impure thoughts is all them bastards ever confess.

COLEMAN. Em, only I don't think you should be telling me what people be confessing, Father. You can be excommunicated for that I think. I saw it in a film with Montgomery Clift.

WELSH. Do ya see? I'm shite sure.

COLEMAN. Too hard on yourself is all you are, and it's only pure gossip that Mick and Maureen murdered anybody, and nothing but gossip. Mick's missus was a pure drink-driving accident is unfortunate but could've happened to anybody....

WELSH. With the scythe hanging out of her forehead, now, Coleman?

COLEMAN. A pure drink-driving, and Maureen's mam only fell down a big hill and Maureen's mam was never steady on her feet.

WELSH. And was even less steady with the brains pouring out of her, a poker swipe.

COLEMAN. She had a bad hip and everybody knew, and if it's at anybody you should be pegging murder accusations, isn't it me? Shot me dad's head off him, point blank range.

WELSH. Aye, but an accident that was, and you had a witness....

COLEMAN. Is what I'm saying. And if Valene hadn't happened to be there to see me tripping and the gun falling, wouldn't the town be saying I put the barrel bang up agin him, blew the head off him on purpose? It's only because poor Mick and Maureen had no witnesses is why all them gobshites do go gossiping about them. *(Valene returns with his pen and starts drawing 'V's on the new figurines.)*

WELSH. See? You do see the good in people, Coleman. That's what I'm supposed to do, but I don't. I'm always at the head of the queue to be pegging the first stone.

VALENE. He's not having another fecking crisis of faith?

COLEMAN. He is.

VALENE. He never stops, this fella.

WELSH. Aye, because I have nothing to offer me parish at all.

COLEMAN. Sure haven't you just coached the under-twelves football to the Connaught semifinals yere first year trying?

WELSH. Ah the under-twelves football isn't enough to restore your faith in the priesthood, Coleman, and we're a bunch of foulers anyway.

COLEMAN. Ye aren't. Ye're skillful.

WELSH. Ten red cards in four games, Coleman. That's a world's record in girls' football. That'd be a record in boys' football. One of the lasses from St. Angela's she's still in hospital after meeting us.

COLEMAN. If she wasn't up for the job she shouldn't've been on the field of play.

WELSH. Them poor lasses used to go off crying. Oh a great coach I am, oh aye.

11

COLEMAN.   Sissy whining bitches is all them little feckers are.
(A rap on the front door, then Girleen, a pretty girl of seventeen, puts her head round it.)
GIRLEEN.   Are ye in need?
VALENE.   Come in for yourself, Girleen. I'll be taking a couple of bottles off ya, aye. I'll get me money. *(Valene exits to his room as Girleen enters, taking two bottles of poteen out of her bag.)*
GIRLEEN.   Coleman. Father Welsh Walsh Welsh....
WELSH.   Welsh.
GIRLEEN.   Welsh. I know. Don't be picking me up. How is all?
COLEMAN.   We've just stuck our dad in the ground.
GIRLEEN.   Grand, grand. I met the postman on the road with a letter for Valene. *(She lays an official-looking envelope on table.)* That postman fancies me, d'you know? I think he'd like to be getting into me knickers, in fact I'm sure of it.
COLEMAN.   Him and the rest of Galway, Girleen. *(Welsh puts his head in his hands at this talk.)*
GIRLEEN.   Galway minimum. The EC more like. Well, a fella won't be getting into my knickers on a postman's wages. I'll tell you that, now.
COLEMAN.   Are you charging for entry so, Girleen?
GIRLEEN.   I'm tinkering with the idea, Coleman. Why, are you interested? It'll take more than a pint and a bag of Taytos, mind.
COLEMAN.   I have a three-pound postal order somewhere I never used.
GIRLEEN.   That's nearer the mark, now. *(To Welsh.)* What kind of wages do priests be on, Father?
WELSH.   Will you stop now?! Will you stop?! Isn't it enough for a girl going round flogging poteen, not to go talking about whoring herself on top of it?!
GIRLEEN.   Ah, we're only codding you, Father. *(She fluffs her fingers through Welsh's hair. He brushes her off. To Coleman.)* He's not having another crisis of faith is he? That's twelve this week. We should report him to Jesus. *(Walsh moans into his hands. Girleen giggles slightly. Valene enters and pays Girleen.)*
VALENE.   Two bottles, Girleen.
GIRLEEN.   Two bottles it is. You've a letter there.
COLEMAN.   Buy me a bottle, Valene. I'll owe ya.

VALENE. *(Opening letter.)* Buy you a bottle me arse.

COLEMAN. Do you see this fella?

GIRLEEN. You've diddled me out of a pound, Valene. *(Valene pays up as if expecting it.)*

VALENE. It was worth a go.

GIRLEEN. You're the king of stink-scum fecking filth-bastards you, ya bitch-feck, Valene.

WELSH. Don't be swearing like that now, Girleen....

GIRLEEN. Ah me hairy arse, Father.

VALENE. *(Re letter.)* Yes! It's here! It's here! Me cheque! And look how much too! *(Valene holds the cheque up in front of Coleman's face.)*

COLEMAN. I see how much.

VALENE. Do ya see?

COLEMAN. I see now, and out of me face take it.

VALENE. *(Holding it closer.)* Do ya see how much, now?

COLEMAN. I see now.

VALENE. And all to me. Is it a closer look you do need?

COLEMAN. Out of me face take that thing now.

VALENE. But maybe it's closer you need to be looking now.... *(Valene rubs the cheque in Coleman's face. Coleman jumps up and grabs Valene by the neck. Valene grabs him in the same way. Girleen laughs as they struggle together. Welsh darts drunkenly across and breaks the two apart.)*

WELSH. Be stopping, now! What's the matter with ye? *(Welsh gets accidentally kicked as the brothers part. He winces.)*

COLEMAN. I'm sorry, Father. I was aiming at that feck.

WELSH. Hurt that did! Bang on me fecking shin.

GIRLEEN. You'll know now how the lasses at St. Angela's be feeling.

WELSH. What's the matter with ye at all, sure?

VALENE. He started it.

WELSH. Two brothers laying into each other the same day their father was buried! I've never heard the like.

GIRLEEN. It's all because you're such a terrible priest to them, Father. *(Welsh glares at her. She looks away, smiling.)* I'm only codding you, Father.

WELSH. What kind of a town is this at all? Brothers fighting

13

and lasses peddling booze and two fecking murderers on the loose?

GIRLEEN. And me pregnant on top of it. *(Pause.)* I'm not really. *(Welsh looks at her and them sadly, moving somewhat drunkenly to the door.)*

WELSH. Don't be fighting any more, now, ye's two. *(Exits.)*

GIRLEEN. Father Walsh Welsh has no sense of humour. I'll walk him the road home for himself, and see he doesn't get hit be a cow like the last time.

COLEMAN. See you so, Girleen.

VALENE. See you so, Girleen. *(Girleen exits. Pause.)* That fella, eh?

COLEMAN. *(In agreement.)* Eh? That fella.

VALENE. Jeez. Eh? If he found out you blew the head off dad on purpose, he'd probably get three times as maudlin.

COLEMAN. He takes things too much to heart does that fella.

VALENE. Way too much to heart. *(Blackout.)*

Scene 2

Evening. Against the back wall and blocking out the fire-place is now situated a large, new orange stove with a big 'V' scrawled on its front. Coleman, in glasses, sits in the armchair left, reading Woman's Own, *a glass of poteen beside him. Valene enters, carrying a bag. Slowly, deliberately, he places a hand on the stove in a number of places in case it's been used recently. Coleman snorts in disgust at him.*

VALENE. I'm checking.

COLEMAN. I can see you're checking.

VALENE. I like to have a little check with you around.

COLEMAN. That's what you do best is check.

VALENE. Just a biteen of a check, like. D'you know what I

14

mean? In *my* opinion, like.

COLEMAN.   I wouldn't touch your stove if you shoved a kettle up me arse.

VALENE.   Is right, my stove.

COLEMAN.   If you fecking paid me I wouldn't touch your stove.

VALENE.   Well I won't be fecking paying you to touch me stove.

COLEMAN.   I know well you won't, you tight-fisted feck.

VALENE.   And *my* stove is right. Did *you* pay the three hundred? Did *you* get the gas fixed up? No. Who did? Me. My money. Was it your money? No, it was my money.

COLEMAN.   I know well it was your money.

VALENE.   If you'd made a contribution I'd've said go ahead and use me stove, but you didn't, so I won't.

COLEMAN.   We don't even need a stove.

VALENE.   You may not need a stove, but I need a stove.

COLEMAN.   You never fecking eat, sure!

VALENE.   I'll start! Aye, by Christ I'll start. *(Pause.)* This stove is mine, them figurines are mine, this gun, them chairs, that table's mine. What else? This floor, them cupboards, everything in this fecking house is mine, and you don't go touching, boy. Not without me express permission.

COLEMAN.   It'll be hard not to touch your fecking floor, now.

VALENE.   Not without me express....

COLEMAN.   Unless I go fecking levitating.

VALENE.   Not without me express....

COLEMAN.   Like them darkies.

VALENE.   *(Angrily.)* Not without me express fecking permission I'm saying!

COLEMAN.   Your express permission, oh aye.

VALENE.   To *me* all this was left. To me and me alone.

COLEMAN.   Twasn't left but twas *awarded.*

VALENE.   Me and me alone.

COLEMAN.   Awarded it was.

VALENE.   And you don't go touching. *(Pause.)* What darkies?

COLEMAN.   Eh?

VALENE. What darkies go levitating?

COLEMAN. Them darkies. On them carpets. Them levitating darkies.

VALENE. Them's Pakies. Not darkies at all!

COLEMAN. The same differ!

VALENE. Not at all the same differ! Them's Paki-men, same as whistle at the snakes.

COLEMAN. It seems like you're the expert on Paki-men!

VALENE. I *am* the expert on Paki-men!

COLEMAN. You probably go falling in love with Paki-men too, so! Oh I'm sure.

VALENE. Leave falling in love out of it.

COLEMAN. What did you get shopping, Mister 'I-want-to-marry-a-Paki-man'?

VALENE. What did I get shopping, is it? *(Valene takes two figurines out of his bag and arranges them delicately on the shelf.)*

COLEMAN. Ah for feck's sake....

VALENE. Don't be cursing now, Coleman. Not in front of the saints. Against God that is. *(He takes eight packets of Taytos out of the bag and lays them on the table.)* And some Taytos I got.

COLEMAN. Be getting McCoys if you're getting crisps.

VALENE. I'll be getting what I li....

COLEMAN. Ya fecking cheapskate.

VALENE. *(Pause. Glaring.)* I'm not getting some crisps taste exactly the same, cost double, Coleman.

COLEMAN. They don't taste the same and they have grooves.

VALENE. They do taste the same and feck grooves.

COLEMAN. Taytos are dried fecking filth and everybody knows they are.

VALENE. The crisp expert now I'm listening to. What matter if they're dried fecking filth? They're seventeen pee, and whose crisps are they anyways? They're my crisps.

COLEMAN. They're your crisps.

VALENE. My crisps and my crisps alone.

COLEMAN. Or get Ripples.

VALENE. Ripples me arse and I don't see you digging in your ... what's this? *(Valene picks up Coleman's glass and sniffs it.)*

COLEMAN. What's wha?

VALENE. This.

16

COLEMAN. Me own.

VALENE. Your own your arse. You've no money to be getting your own.

COLEMAN. I do have.

VALENE. From where?

COLEMAN. Am I being interrogated now?

VALENE. You are.

COLEMAN. Feck ya so. *(Valene takes his poteen out of his biscuit tin to check if any is missing. Coleman puts the magazine aside, takes his glasses off and sits at the table.)*

VALENE. You've been at this.

COLEMAN. I haven't at all been at that.

VALENE. It seems very ... reduced.

COLEMAN. Reduced me arse. I wouldn't be at yours if you shoved a fecking....

VALENE. *(Sipping it, uncertain.)* You've topped it up with water.

COLEMAN. Be believing what you wish. I never touched your poteen.

VALENE. Where would you get money for.... Me house insurance?! Oh you fecker...! *(Valene desperately finds and examines his insurance book.)*

COLEMAN. I paid in your house insurance.

VALENE. This isn't Duffy's signature.

COLEMAN. It is Duffy's signature. Doesn't it say 'Duffy'?

VALENE. You paid it?

COLEMAN. Aye.

VALENE. Why?

COLEMAN. Oh to do you a favour, after all the favours you've done me over the years. Oh aye.

VALENE. It's easy enough to check.

COLEMAN. It *is* easy enough to check, and check ahead, ya feck. Check until you're blue in the face. *(Confused, Valene puts the book away.)* It's not only money can buy you booze. No. Sex appeal it is too.

VALENE. Sex appeal? You? Your sex appeal wouldn't buy the phlegm off a dead frog.

COLEMAN. You have your own opinion and you're well entitled to it. Girleen's of the opposite opinion.

VALENE. Girleen? Me arse.

COLEMAN. Is true.

VALENE. Eh?

COLEMAN. I said let me have a bottle on tick and I'll be giving you a big kiss, now. She said 'If you let me be touching you below, sure you can have a bottle for nothing.' The deal was struck then and there.

VALENE. Girleen wouldn't touch you below if you bought her a pony, let alone giving poteen away on top of it.

COLEMAN. I can only be telling the God's honest truth, and how else would I be getting poteen for free?

VALENE. *(Unsure.)* Me arse. *(Pause.)* Eh? *(Pause.)* Girleen's pretty. *(Pause.)* Girleen's awful pretty. *(Pause.)* Why would Girleen be touching you below?

COLEMAN. Mature men it is Girleen likes.

VALENE. I don't believe you at all.

COLEMAN. Don't so.

VALENE. *(Pause.)* What did it feel like?

COLEMAN. What did what feel like?

VALENE. The touching below.

COLEMAN. Em, nice enough now.

VALENE. *(Unsure.)* I don't believe you at all. (Pause.) No, I don't believe you at all. *(Coleman opens and starts eating a packet of Valene's crisps.)* Girleen wouldn't be touching you below. Never in the world would Girleen be touching y.... *(Stunned.)* Who said you could go eating me crisps?!

COLEMAN. Nobody said.

VALENE. In front of me?!

COLEMAN. I decided of me own accord.

VALENE. You'll be paying me seventeen pee of your own accord so! And right now you'll be paying me!

COLEMAN. Right now, is it?

VALENE. It is!

COLEMAN. The money you have stashed?

VALENE. And if you don't pay up it's a batter I'll be giving you.

COLEMAN. A batter from you? I'd be as scared of a batter from a lemon.

VALENE. Seventeen pee I'm saying. *(Pause. Coleman slowly takes*

18

a coin out of his pocket and, without looking at it, slams it down on the table. Valene looks at the coin.) That's ten. *(Coleman looks at the coin, takes out another one and slams that down also.)*

COLEMAN.   You can keep the change.

VALENE.   I can keep the change, can I? *(He pockets the coins, takes out three pee, opens one of Coleman's hands and places the money in it.)* I'm in no need of charity. *(He turns away. Still sitting, Coleman throws the coins hard at the back of Valene's head.)* Ya fecker ya!! Come on so! *(Coleman jumps up, knocking his chair over.)*

COLEMAN.   Come on so, is it?

VALENE.   Pegging good money at me?!

COLEMAN.   It is. And be picking that money up now, for your oul piggy-bank, ya little virgin fecking gayboy ya.... *(The two grapple, fall to the floor and roll around scuffling. Welsh enters through the front door, slightly drunk.)*

WELSH.   Hey ye's two! Ye's two! *(Pause. Loudly.)* Ye's two!

COLEMAN.   *(Irritated.)* Wha?

WELSH.   Tom Hanlon's just killed himself.

VALENE.   Eh?

WELSH.   Tom Hanlon's just killed himself.

VALENE.   *(Pause.)* Let go o'me neck, you.

COLEMAN.   Let go o'me arm so. *(The two slowly let go of each other and stand up, as Welsh sits at the table, stunned.)*

WELSH.   He walked out into the lake from the oul jetty there. Aye, and kept walking. His body's on the shingle. His father had to haul me drunk out of Rory's to say a prayer o'er him, and me staggering.

VALENE.   Tom Hanlon? Jeez. Sure I was only talking to Tom a day ago there. The funeral.

WELSH.   A child seen him. Seen him sitting on the bench on the jetty, a pint with him, looking out across the lake to the mountains there. And when his pint was done he got up and started walking, the clothes still on him, and didn't stop walking. No. 'Til the poor head of him was under. And even then he didn't stop.

COLEMAN.   *(Pause.)* Ah I never liked that Tom fecking Hanlon. He was always full of himself, same as all fecking coppers....

WELSH.   *(Angrily.)* The poor man's not even cold yet, Coleman

19

Connor. Do you have to be talking that way about him?

COLEMAN. I do, or if I'm not to be a hypocrite anyways I do.

VALENE. It's hypocrites now. Do you see this fella, Father? Ate a bag of me crisps just now without a by your leave....

COLEMAN. I paid you for them crisps....

VALENE. Then says he's not a hypocrite.

COLEMAN. I paid thruppence over the odds for them crisps, and how does eating crisps make you a hypocrite anyways?

VALENE. It just does. And interfering with a schoolgirl on top of it is another crime, Father.

COLEMAN. I interfered with no schoolgirl. I was interfered with *be* a schoolgirl.

VALENE. The same differ!

WELSH. What schoolgirl's this, now?

COLEMAN. Girleen this schoolgirl is. This afternoon there she came up and a fine oul time we had, oh aye.

WELSH. Girleen? Sure Girleen's been helping me wash the strips for the under-twelves football all day, never left me sight. *(Embarrassed, Coleman gets up and moves towards his room. Valene blocks his way.)*

VALENE. Aha! Aha! Now who's the virgin fecking gayboy, eh? Now who's the virgin fecking gayboy?

COLEMAN. Out of me way, now.

VALENE. *Now*, eh?

COLEMAN. Out of me way I'm saying.

VALENE. I knew well!

COLEMAN. Are you moving or am I moving ya?

VALENE. *Now* did I know well? Eh?

COLEMAN. Eh?

VALENE. Eh?

WELSH. Coleman, come back now. We....

COLEMAN. And you can shut your fecking gob too, Welsh or Walsh or whatever your fecking name is, ya priest! You don't go catching Coleman Connor out on lies and expect to be ... and be expecting to ... to be.... *(Coleman enters his room, slamming its door.)*

VALENE. You're a stuttering oul ass, so you are! 'To be ... to be ... to be....' *(To Welsh.)* Eh? *(As Valene turns back to Welsh, Coleman*

20

dashes out, kicks the stove and dashes back to his room, Valene trying and failing to catch him.) Ya fecker, ya! *(He checks the stove for damage.)* Me good fecking stove! If there's any damage done to this stove it'll be you'll be paying for it, ya feck! Did you see that, Father? Isn't that man mad? *(Pause.)* Do ya like me new stove, Father? Isn't it a good one?

COLEMAN. *(Off.)* Do ya see that 'V' on his stove, Father? Do you think it's a V for Valene? It isn't. It's a V for Virgin, it is.

VALENE. Oh is it now...?

COLEMAN. *(Off.)* V for virgin it is, uh-huh.

VALENE. When you're the king of the virgins?

COLEMAN. *(Off.)* Valene the Virgin that V stands for.

VALENE. The fecking king of them you are! And don't be listening at doors!

COLEMAN. *(Off.)* I'll be doing what I wish. *(Valene checks stove again. Welsh is on the verge of tears.)*

VALENE. *(Re stove.)* No, I think it's okay, now....

WELSH. You see, I come in to ye ... and ye're fighting. Fair enough, now, that's all ye two ever do is fight. Ye'll never be changed. It's enough times I've tried....

VALENE. Are you crying, Father, or is it a bit of a cold you do have? Ah it's a cold....

WELSH. It's crying I am.

VALENE. Well I've never seen the like.

WELSH. Cos I come in, and I tell ya a fella's just gone and killed himself, a fella ye went to school with ... a fella ye grew up with ... a fella never had a bad word to say about anybody and did his best to be serving the community every day of his life ... and I tell you he's killed himself be drowning, is a horrible way to die, and not only do ye not bat an eye ... not only do ye not bat an eye but ye go arguing about crisps and stoves then!

VALENE. I batted an eye.

WELSH. I didn't notice that eye batted!

VALENE. I batted a big eye.

WELSH. Well I didn't notice it, now!

VALENE. *(Pause.)* But isn't it a nice stove, Father? *(Welsh puts his head in his hands. Valene goes to the stove.)* Only a day I've had it fixed up. You can still smell as clean as it is. Coleman's forbid to touch it at all because Coleman didn't contribute a penny towards it, for Coleman doesn't *have* a penny to contribute towards it. *(Picks up the three pee.)* He has three pee, but three pee won't go too far towards a stove. Not too far at all. He threw this three pee at me head earlier, d'you know? *(In realisation, angrily.)* And if he has no money and he wasn't interfered with, where the feck was it that poteen did come from?! Coleman...!

WELSH. *(Screams.)* Valene, you fecking fecker ya!!

VALENE. What? Oh, aye, poor Thomas. *(Valene nods in phony empathy.)*

WELSH. *(Pause. Sadly, standing.)* I came up to get ye to come to the lake with me, to be dragging poor Tom's body home for himself. Will ye be helping now?

VALENE. I will be, Father. I will be.

WELSH. *(Pause.)* Feck. Two murders and a suicide now. Two murders and a fecking suicide.... *(Welsh exits, shaking his head.)*

VALENE. *(Calling out.)* Sure, not your fault was it, Father. Don't you be getting maudlin again! *(Pause.)* Coleman? I'm off down....

COLEMAN. *(Off.)* I heard.

VALENE. Are ya coming so?

COLEMAN. *(Off.)* Not at all am I coming. To go humping a dead policeman about the country? A dead policeman used to laugh at me press-ups in PE? I don't fecking think so, now.

VALENE. You forever bear a grudge, you. Ah anyways it's good strong men Father Walsh does need helping him, not virgin fecking gayboys couldn't pay a drunk monkey to go interfering with him. *(Valene quickly exits. Coleman storms into the room to find him gone. He goes to the door and idles there, thinking, looking around the room. His gaze falls on the stove. He picks up some matches and opens the stove door.)*

COLEMAN. A virgin fecking gayboy, is it? Shall we be having gas mark ten for no reason at all, now? We shall, d'you know? *(He lights the stove, turns it up, closes its door and exits to his room. He returns a few seconds later and looks around the room.)* For no reason at all, is it? *(He takes a large oven-proof bowl out of the cupboard, places all of the figurines from the shelf into the bowl and puts the bowl inside the stove, closing its door afterwards.)* Now we'll be seeing who's a virgin gayboy couldn't pay a monkey to interfere with him. I'll say we'll fecking see. *(He pulls on his jacket, brushes his unkempt hair for two seconds with a manky comb, and exits through the front door. Blackout.)*

Scene 3

A few hours later. Valene and Welsh enter, slightly drunk. Valene takes his poteen out of his tin and pours himself a glass. Welsh eyes it a little.

VALENE.   That was an awful business, eh?

WELSH.   Terrible. Just terrible, now. And I couldn't say a thing to them. Not a thing.

VALENE.   What could be said to them, sure? The only thing they wanted to hear was 'Your son isn't dead at all', and that wouldn't have worked. Not with him lying in their front room, dripping.

WELSH.   Did you ever hear such crying, Valene?

VALENE.   You could've filled a lake with the tears that family cried. Or a russaway at a minimum.

WELSH.   *(Pause.)* A wha?

VALENE.   A russaway. One of them russaways.

WELSH.   Reservoir?

VALENE.   Russaway, aye, and their Mairtin crying with the best of them. I've never seen Mairtin crying as hard. I suppose that's all you deserve for chopping the ears off a poor dog.

WELSH.   I suppose if it's your only brother you lose you do cry hard.

VALENE.   I wouldn't cry hard if I lost me only brother. I'd buy a big cake and have a crowd round.

WELSH.   Ah Valene, now. If it's your own brother you can't get on with, how can we ever hope for peace in the world...?

VALENE.   Peace me arse and don't keep going on, you. You always do whine on this oul subject when you're drunk. *(Valene sits at the table with drink and bottle).*

23

WELSH. *(Pause.)* A lonesome oul lake that is for a fella to go killing himself in. It makes me sad just to think of it. To think of poor Tom sitting alone there, alone with his thoughts, the cold lake in front of him, and him weighing up what's best, a life full of the loneliness that took him there but a life full of good points too. Every life has good points, even if it's only ... seeing rivers, or going travelling, or watching football on telly....

VALENE. *(Nodding.)* Football, aye....

WELSH. Or the hopes of being loved. And Thomas weighing all that up on the one hand, then weighing up a death in cold water on the other, and choosing the water. And first it strikes you as dumb, and a waste, 'You were thirty-eight years old, you had health and friends, there was plenty worse off fecks than you in the world, Tom Hanlon'....

VALENE. The girl born with no lips in Norway.

WELSH. I didn't hear about her.

VALENE. There was this girl in Norway, and she was born with no lips at all.

WELSH. Uh-huh. But then you say if the world's such a decent place worth staying in, where were his friends when he needed them in this decent world? When he needed them most, to say 'Come away from there, ya daft, we'd miss ya, you're worthwhile, as dumb as you are.' Where were his friends? Where was I then? Sitting pissed on me own in a pub. *(Pause.)* Rotting in hell now, Tom Hanlon is. According to the Catholic Church anyways he is, the same as every suicide. No remorse. No mercy on him.

VALENE. Is that right now? Every suicide you're saying?

WELSH. According to us mob it's right anyways.

VALENE. Well I didn't know that. That's a turn-up for the books. *(Pause.)* So the fella from *Alias Smith and Jones*, he'd be in hell?

WELSH. I don't know the fella from *Alias Smith and Jones*.

VALENE. Not the blond one, now, the other one.

WELSH. I don't know the fella.

VALENE. He killed himself, and at the height of his fame.

WELSH. Well if he killed himself, aye, he'll be in hell too. *(Pause.)* It's great it is. You can kill a dozen fellas, you can kill two dozen fellas. So long as you're sorry after you can still get

24

into heaven. But if it's yourself you go murdering, no. Straight to hell.

VALENE. That sounds awful harsh. *(Pause.)* So Tom'll be in hell now, he will? Jeez. *(Pause.)* I wonder if he's met the fella from *Alias Smith and Jones* yet? Ah, that fella must be old be now. Tom probably wouldn't even recognise him. That's if he saw *Alias Smith and Jones* at all. I only saw it in England. It mightn't've been on telly here at all.

WELSH. *(Sighing.)* You wouldn't be sparing a drop of that poteen would ya, Valene? I've an awful thirst....

VALENE. Ah, Father, I have only a drop left and I need that for meself....

WELSH. You've half the bottle, sure....

VALENE. And if I had some I'd spare it, but I don't, and should priests be going drinking anyways? No they shouldn't, or anyways not on the night....

WELSH. Thou shouldst share and share alike the Bible says. Or somewhere it says....

VALENE. Not on the night you let one of your poor flock go murdering himself you shouldn't, is what me sentence was gong to be.

WELSH. Well was that a nice thing to be saying?! Do I need that, now?!

VALENE. *(Mumbling.)* Don't go trying to go cadging a poor fella's drink off him so, the wages you're on. *(Valene gets up, puts the bottle back in his biscuit tin and carefully Sellotapes the lid up, humming as he does so.)*

WELSH. Is there a funny smell off of your house tonight, Val, now?

VALENE. If you're going criticising the smell of me house you can be off now, so you can.

WELSH. Like of plastic, now?

VALENE. Cadging me booze and then saying me house smells. That's the best yet, that is.

WELSH. *(Pause.)* At least Coleman came down to help us with poor Thomas after all, even if he was late. But that was awful wrong of him to go asking Tom's poor mam if she'd be doing vol-au-vents after.

VALENE.   That was awful near the mark.

WELSH.   And her sitting there crying, and him nudging her then, and again and again 'Will ye be having vol-au-vents, Missus, will ye?'

VALENE.   If he was drunk you could excuse it, but he wasn't. It was just out of spite. *(Laughing.)* Although it was funny, now.

WELSH.   Where is he anyways? I thought he was walking the road with us.

VALENE.   He'd stopped to do up his shoelaces a way back. *(Pause. In realisation.)* Coleman *has* no shoelaces. He has only loafers. *(Pause.)* Where have all me Virgin Marys gone?! *(He leans in over the stove, placing his hands on its top, to see if the figurines have fallen down the back. The searing heat from the stove burns his hands and he pulls them away, yelping. Hysterical.)* Wha?! Wha?!

WELSH.   What is it, Valene? Did you go leaving your stove on? *(Stunned, Valene opens the stove door with a towel. Smoke billows out. He takes the steaming bowl of molten plastic out, sickened, places it on the table and delicately picks up one of the half-melted figurines with the towel.)* All your figurines are melted, Valene.

VALENE.   *(Staggering backwards.)* I'll kill the feck! I'll kill the feck!

WELSH.   I'll be betting it was Coleman, Valene.

VALENE.   That's all there is to it! I'll kill the feck! *(Valene pulls the shotgun off the wall and marches around the room in a daze, as Welsh jumps up and tries to calm him.)*

WELSH.   Oh Valene now! Put that gun down!

VALENE.   I'll blow the head off him! The fecking head off him I'll blow! I tell him not to touch me stove and I tell him not to touch me figurines and what does he do? He cooks me figurines in me stove! *(Looking into bowl.)* That one was blessed be the Pope! That one was given me mammy be Yanks! And they're all gone! All of them! They're all just the fecking heads and bobbing around!

WELSH.   You can't go shooting your brother o'er inanimate objects, Valene! Give me that gun, now.

VALENE.   Inanimate objects? Me figurines of the saints? And you call yoursel' a priest? No wonder you're the laughing stock of the Catholic Church in Ireland. And that takes some fecking doing, boy.

WELSH. Give it me now, I'm saying. Your own flesh and blood this is you're talking of murdering.

VALENE. Me own flesh and blood is right, and why not? If he's allowed to murder his own flesh and blood and get away with it, why shouldn't I be?

WELSH. What are you talking about, now? Coleman shooting your dad was a pure accident and you know well.

VALENE. A pure accident me arse! You're the only fecker in Leenane believes that shooting was an accident. Didn't Dad make a jibe about Coleman's hairstyle, and didn't Coleman dash out, pull him back be the hair and blow the poor skulleen out his head, the same as he'd been promising to do since the age of eight and Da trod on his Scalectrix, broke it in two.... *(Coleman enters through the front door.)*

COLEMAN. Well I did love that Scalectrix. It had glow in the dark headlamps. *(Valene turns and points the gun at Coleman. Welsh backs off moaning, hands to his head. Coleman nonchalantly idles to the table and sits down.)*

WELSH. It can't be true! It can't be true!

COLEMAN. Look at that fella gone pure white....

VALENE. No, shut up you! Don't be coming in mouthing after your fecking crimes....

WELSH. Tell me you didn't shoot your dad on purpose, Coleman. Please, now....

VALENE. This isn't about our fecking dad! This is about me fecking figurines!

COLEMAN. Do you see this fella's priorities?

VALENE. Melting figurines is against God outright!

WELSH. So is shooting your dad in the head, sure!

VALENE. And on gas mark ten!

WELSH. Tell me, Coleman, tell me, please. Tell me you didn't shoot your dad there on purpose. Oh tell me, now....

COLEMAN. Will you calm down, you? *(Pause.)* Of course I shot me dad on purpose. *(Welsh starts groaning again.)* I don't take criticising from nobody. 'Me hair's like a drunken child's.' I'd only just combed me hair and there was nothing wrong with it! And I know well shooting your dad in the head is against God, but there's some insults that can never be excused.

VALENE. And cooking figurines is against God on top of it, if they're Virgin Mary figurines anyways.

COLEMAN. Is true enough, be the fella with the gun, and I'll tell you another thing that's against God, before this fella puts a bullet in me.... *(To Welsh.)* Hey moany, are you listening...?

WELSH. I'm listening, I'm listening, I'm listening....

COLEMAN. I'll tell you another thing that's against God. Sitting your brother in a chair, with his dad's brains dripping down him, and promising to tell everyone it was nothing but an accident....

VALENE. Shut up now, ya feck....

COLEMAN. So long as there and then you sign over everything your dad went and left you in his will....

WELSH. No ... no ... no....

COLEMAN. His house and his land and his tables and his chairs and his bit of money to go frittering away on shitey-arsed ovens you only got to torment me, ya feck....

WELSH. No, now ... no....

VALENE. Be saying good-bye to the world, you, fecker!

COLEMAN. And fecking Taytos then, the worst crisps in the world.... *(Valene cocks the gun that's up against Coleman's head.)*

WELSH. No, Valene, no!

VALENE. I said say good-bye to the world, ya feck.

COLEMAN. Good-bye to the world, ya feck. *(Valene pulls the trigger. There is a hollow click. He pulls the trigger again. Another click. A third time, and another click, as Coleman reaches in his pocket and takes out two shotgun cartridges.)* Do you think I'm fecking stupid, now? *(To Welsh.)* Did you see that, Father? My own brother going shooting me in the head.

VALENE. Give me them fecking bullets, now.

COLEMAN. No.

VALENE. Give me them bullets I'm saying.

COLEMAN. I won't.

VALENE. Give me them fecking.... *(Valene tries to wrench the bullets out of Coleman's clenched fist, Coleman laughing as he does so.*

28

Valene grabs Coleman by the neck and they fall to the floor, grappling, rolling around the place. Welsh stares at the two of them dumbstruck, horrified. He catches sight of the bowl of steaming plastic beside him and, almost blankly, as the grappling continues, clenches his fists and slowly lowers them into the burning liquid, holding them under. Through clenched teeth and without breathing, Welsh manages to withhold his screaming for about ten or fifteen seconds until, still holding his fists under, he lets rip with a horrifying high-pitched wail lasting about ten seconds, during which Valene and Coleman stop fighting, stand, and try to help him....) Father Walsh, now ...

COLEMAN.   Father Walsh, Father Walsh.... *(Welsh pulls his fists out of the bowl, red raw, stifles his screams again, looks over the shocked Valene and Coleman in despair and torment, smashes the bowl off the table and dashes out through the front door, his fists clutched to his check in pain.)*

WELSH.   *(Exiting, screaming.)* Me name's *Welsh!!! (Valene and Coleman stare after him a moment or two.)*

COLEMAN.   Sure that fella's pure mad.

VALENE.   He's outright mad.

COLEMAN.   He's a lube. *(Gesturing at bowl.)* Will he be expecting us to clear his mess up? *(Valene puts his head out the front door and calls out.)*

VALENE.   Will you be expecting us to clear your mess up, you?

COLEMAN.   *(Pause.)* What did he say?

VALENE.   He was gone.

COLEMAN.   A lube and nothing but a lube. *(Pause.)* Ah it's your fecking floor. You clean it up.

VALENE.   You wha?!

COLEMAN.   Do you see me nice bullets, Valene? *(Coleman rattles his two bullets in Valene's face, then exits to his room.)*

VALENE.   Ya fecking...! *(Coleman's door slams shut. Valene grimaces, pauses, scratches his balls blankly and sniffs his fingers. Pause. Blackout. Interval.)*

Scene 1

A plain bench on a lakeside jetty at night, on which Welsh sits with a pint, his hands lightly bandaged. Girleen comes over and sits down beside him.

WELSH.   Girleen.

GIRLEEN.   Father. What are ya up to?

WELSH.   Just sitting here, now.

GIRLEEN.   Oh aye, aye. *(Pause.)* That was a nice sermon at Thomas's today, Father.

WELSH.   I didn't see you there, did I?

GIRLEEN.   I was at the back a ways. *(Pause.)* Almost made me go crying, them words did.

WELSH.   You crying? I've never in all the years heard of you going crying, Girleen. Not at funerals, not at weddings. You didn't even cry when Holland knocked us out of the fecking World Cup.

GIRLEEN.   Now and then on me now I go crying, over different things....

WELSH.   That Packie fecking Bonner. He couldn't save a shot from a fecking cow. *(Welsh sips his pint.)*

GIRLEEN.   I'd be saying you've had a few now, Father?

WELSH.   Don't you be starting on me now. On top of everybody else.

GIRLEEN.   I wasn't starting on ya.

WELSH.   Not today, of all days.

GIRLEEN.   I wasn't starting at all on ya. I do tease you sometimes but that's all I do do.

WELSH.   Sometimes, is it? All the time, more like, the same as everybody round here.

GIRLEEN.   I do only tease you now and again, and only to cam ouflage the mad passion I have deep within me for ya.... *(Welsh*

30

gives her a dirty look. She smiles.) No, I'm only joking now, Father.

WELSH. Do ya see?!

GIRLEEN. Ah be taking a joke will ya, Father? It's only cos you're so high-horse and up yourself that you make such an easy target.

WELSH. I'm not so high-horse and up meself.

GIRLEEN. All right you're not so.

WELSH. *(Pause.) Am* I so high-horse and up meself?

GIRLEEN. No, now. Well, no more than most priests.

WELSH. Maybe I am high-horse so. Maybe that's why I don't fit into this town. Although I'd have to have killed half me fecking relatives to fit into this town. Jeez. I thought Leenane was a nice place when first I turned up here, but no. Turns out it's the murder capital of fecking Europe. Did *you* know Coleman had killed his dad on purpose?

GIRLEEN. *(Lowers head, embarrassed.)* I think I did hear a rumour somewhere along the line....

WELSH. A fecking rumour? And you didn't bat an eye or go reporting it?

GIRLEEN. Sure I'm no fecking stool-pigeon and Coleman's dad was always a grumpy oul feck. He did kick me cat Eamonn there once.

WELSH. A fella deserves to die, so, for kicking a cat?

GIRLEEN. *(Shrugs.)* It depends on the fella. And the cat. But there'd be a lot less cats kicked in Ireland, I'll tell ya, if the fella could rest-assured he'd be shot in the head after.

WELSH. You have no morals at all, it seems, Girleen.

GIRLEEN. I have plenty of morals only I don't keep whining on about them like some fellas.

WELSH. *(Pause.)* Val and Coleman'll kill each other someday if somebody doesn't do something to stop them. It won't be me who stops them anyways. It'll be someone with guts for the job. *(He takes out a letter and passes it to Girleen.)* I've written them a little lettereen here, Girleen, would you give it to them next time you see them?

GIRLEEN. Won't you be seeing them soon enough yourself?

WELSH. I won't be. I'm leaving Leenane tonight.

GIRLEEN. Leaving for where?

WELSH. Anywhere. Wherever they send me. Anywhere but here.

GIRLEEN. But why, Father?

WELSH. Ah lots of different reasons, now, but the three slaughterings and one suicide amongst me congregation didn't help.

GIRLEEN. But none of that was your fault, Father.

WELSH. Oh no?

GIRLEEN. And don't you have the under-twelves semifinal tomorrow morning to be coaching?

WELSH. Them bitches have never listened to me advice before. I don't see why they should go starting now. Nobody ever listens to my advice. Nobody ever listens to me at all.

GIRLEEN. I listen to you.

WELSH. *(Sarcastic.)* Ar that's great comfort. *(Girleen bows her head, hurt.)* And you don't listen to me either. How many times have I told you to stop flogging your dad's booze about town, and still you don't?

GIRLEEN. Ah it's just 'til I save up a few bob, Father, I'm doing that flogging.

WELSH. A few bob for what? To go skittering it away the clubs in Carraroe, and drunk schoolboys pawing at ya.

GIRLEEN. Not at all, Father. I do save it to buy a few nice things out me mam's Freeman's catalogue. They do have an array of....

WELSH. To go buying shite, aye. Well I wish I did have as tough problems in my life as you do in yours, Girleen. It does sound like life's a constant torment for ya. *(Girleen stands up and wrenches Welsh's head back by the hair.)*

GIRLEEN. If anybody else went talking to me that sarcastic I'd punch them in the fecking eye for them, only if I punched you in the fecking eye you'd probably go crying like a fecking girl!

WELSH. I never asked you to come sitting beside me.

GIRLEEN. Well I didn't know there was a law against sitting beside ya, although I wish there fecking was one now. *(Girleen releases him and starts walking away.)*

WELSH. I'm sorry for being sarcastic to you, Girleen, about your mam's catalogue and whatnot. I am. *(Girleen stops, pauses, and idles back to the bench.)*

GIRLEEN. It's okay.

WELSH. It's only that I'm feeling a bit ... I don't know....

GIRLEEN. *(Sitting beside him.)* Maudlin.

WELSH. Maudlin. Maudlin is right.

GIRLEEN. Maudlin and lonesome. The maudlin and lonesome Father Walsh. *Welsh. (Pause.)* I'm sorry, Father.

WELSH. Nobody ever remembers.

GIRLEEN. It's just Walsh is so close to Welsh, Father.

WELSH. I know it is. I know it is.

GIRLEEN. What's your first name, Father?

WELSH. *(Pause.)* Roderick. *(Girleen stifles laughter. Welsh smiles.)*

GIRLEEN. Roderick? *(Pause.)* Roderick's a horrible name, Father.

WELSH. I know, and thanks for saying so, Girleen, but you're just trying to boost me spirits now, aren't ya?

GIRLEEN. I'm just being nice to ya now.

WELSH. What kind of a name's Girleen for a girl anyways? What's your proper first name?

GIRLEEN. *(Cringing.)* Mary.

WELSH. *(Laughing.)* Mary? And you go laughing at Roderick then?

GIRLEEN. Mary's the name of the mammy of Our Lord, did you ever hear tell of it?

WELSH. I heard of it somewhere along the line.

GIRLEEN. It's the reason she never got anywhere for herself. Fecking Mary.

WELSH. *You'll* be getting somewhere for yourself, Girleen.

GIRLEEN. D'ya think so, now?

WELSH. As tough a get as you are? Going threatening to thump priests? Of course. *(Girleen brushes the hair out of Welsh's eyes.)*

GIRLEEN. I wouldn't have gone thumping you, now, Father. *(She gently slaps his cheek.)* Maybe a decent slapeen, now. *(Welsh smiles and faces front. Girleen looks at him, then away, embarrassed.)*

WELSH. *(Pause.)* No, I just came out to have a think about Thomas before I go on me way. Say a little prayer for him.

GIRLEEN. It's tonight you're going?

WELSH. It's tonight, aye. I said to meself I'll stay for Tom's funeral, then that'll be the end of it.

33

GIRLEEN. But that's awful quick. No one'll have a chance to wish you good-bye, Father.

WELSH. Good-bye, aye, and good riddance to the back of me.

GIRLEEN. Not at all.

WELSH. No?

GIRLEEN. No. *(Pause. Welsh nods, unconvinced, and drinks again.)* Will you write to me from where you're going and be giving me your new address, Father?

WELSH. I'll try, Girleen, aye.

GIRLEEN. Just so's we can say hello now and then, now.

WELSH. Aye, I'll try. *(As he speaks, Girleen manages to stifle tears without him noticing.)* This is where he walked in from, d'you know? Poor Tom. Look at as cold and bleak as it is. Do you think it took courage or stupidity for him to walk in, Girleen?

GIRLEEN. Courage.

WELSH. The same as that.

GIRLEEN. And Guinness.

WELSH. *(Laughing.)* The same as that. *(Pause.)* Look at as sad and as quiet and still.

GIRLEEN. It's more than Thomas has killed himself here down the years, d'you know, Father? Three other fellas walked in here, me mam was telling me.

WELSH. Is that right now?

GIRLEEN. Years and years ago this is. Maybe even famine times.

WELSH. Drowned themselves?

GIRLEEN. This is where they all come.

WELSH. We should be scared of their ghosts so but we're not scared. Why's that?

GIRLEEN. You're not scared because you're pissed to the gills. I'm not scared because ... I don't know why. One, because you're here, and two, because ... I don't know. I don't be scared of cemeteries at night either. The opposite of that, I do *like* cemeteries at night.

WELSH. Why, now? Because you're a morbid oul tough?

GIRLEEN. *(Embarrassed throughout.)* Not at all. I'm not a tough. It's because ... even if you're sad or something, or lonely or something, you're still better off than them lost in the ground or in the lake, because ... at least you've got the *chance* of being happy, and even if it's a real little chance, it's more than them dead ones have. And it's not that you're saying 'Hah, I'm better than ye', no, because in the long run it might end up that you have a worse life than ever they had and you'd've been better off as dead as them, there and then. But at least when you're still here there's the *possibility* of happiness, and it's like them dead ones know that, and they're happy for you to have it. They say 'Good luck to ya.' *(Quietly.)* Is the way I see it anyways.

WELSH. You have a million thoughts going on at the back of them big brown eyes of yours.

GIRLEEN. I never knew you did ever notice me big brown eyes. Aren't they gorgeous, now?

WELSH. You'll grow up to be a mighty fine woman one day, Girleen, God bless you. *(Welsh drinks again.)*

GIRLEEN. *(Quietly, sadly.)* One day, aye. *(Pause.)* I'll be carrying on the road home for meself now, Father. Will you be staying or will you be walking with me?

WELSH. I'll be staying a biteen longer for meself, Girleen. I'll be saying that prayer for poor Thomas, now.

GIRLEEN. It's good-bye for a while so.

WELSH. It is. *(Girleen kisses his cheek and they hug. Girleen stands.)* You'll remember to be giving that letter to Valene and Coleman, now, Girleen

GIRLEEN. I will. What's in it, Father? It does sound very mysterious. It wouldn't be packed full of condoms for them, would it?

WELSH. It wouldn't at all, now!

GIRLEEN. Cos, you know, Valene and Coleman'd get no use out of them, unless they went using them on a hen.

WELSH. Girleen, now....

GIRLEEN. And it'd need to be a blind hen.

WELSH. You do have a terrible mouth on ya.

GIRLEEN. Aye, all the better to ... no, I won't be finishing that sentence. Did you hear tell of Valene's new hobby, Father? He's been roaming the entirety of Connemara picking up new figurines of the saints for himself, but only ceramic and china ones won't go melting away on him. Thirty-seven of them at last count he has, and only to go tormenting poor Coleman.

WELSH.   Them two, they're just odd.

GIRLEEN.   They *are* odd. They're the kings of odd. *(Pause.)* See you so, Father.

WELSH.   See you so, Girleen. Or Mary, is it?

GIRLEEN.   If you let me know where you get to I'll write with how the under-twelves get on tomorrow. It may be in the *Tribune* anyways. Under 'Girl decapitated in football match.' *(Welsh nods, half smiles. Girleen idles away.)*

WELSH.   Girleen, now? Thanks for coming sitting next to me. It's meant something to me, it has.

GIRLEEN.   Any time, Father. Any time. *(Girleen exits. Welsh stares out front again.)*

WELSH.   *(Quietly.)* No, not any time, Girleen. Not any time. *(Welsh finishes his pint, puts the glass down, blesses himself and sits there quietly a moment, thinking. Blackout.)*

Scene 5

Stage in darkness apart from Welsh, who recites his letter rapidly.

WELSH.   Dear Valene and Coleman, it is Father Welsh here. I am leaving Leenane for good tonight and I wanted to be saying a few words to you, but I won't be preaching at you for why would I be? It has never worked in the past and it won't work now. All I want to do is be pleading with you as a fella concerned about ye and yere lives, both in this world and the next, and the next won't be too long away for ye's if ye keep going on as mad as ye fecking have been. Coleman, I will not be speaking here about your murdering of your dad, although obviously it does concern me, both as a priest and as a person with even the vaguest moral sense, but that is a matter for your own conscience, although I hope some day you will realise what you have done and go seeking forgiveness for it, because let me tell you this, getting your hairstyle insulted is no just cause to go murdering someone, in fact it's the worst cause I did ever hear. But I will leave it at that although the same goes for you, Valene, for your part in your dad's murdering, and don't go saying you had no part because you did have a part and a big part. Going lying that it was an accident just to get your father's money is just as dark a deed as Coleman's deed, if not more dark, for Coleman's deed was done out of temper and spite, whereas your deed was done out of being nothing but a money-grubbing fecking miser with no heart at all, but I said I would not be preaching at you and I have lost me thread anyways so I will stop preaching at you and be starting a new paragraph. *(Pause.)* Like I said, I am leaving tonight, but I have been thinking about ye non-stop since the night I did scald me hands there at yeres. Every time the pain does go through them hands I do think about ye, and let me tell you this. I would take that pain and pain a thousand times worse, and bear it with a smile, if only I could restore to ye the love for each other as brothers ye do so woefully lack, that must have been there some day. Didn't as gasurs ye love each other? Or as young men, now? Where did it all go on ye? Don't ye ever think about it? What I think I think what ye've done is bury it deep down in ye, under a rack of grudges and hate and sniping like a pair of fecking oul women. Ye two are like a pair of fecking oul women, so ye are, arging over fecking Taytos and stoves and figurines, is an arse-brained argument. But I do think that yere love is still there under all of that, in fact I'd go betting everything that's dear to me on it, and may I rot in hell for ever if I'm wrong. All it is is ye've lived in each other's pockets the entire of yere lives, and a sad and lonesome existence it has been, with no women to enter the picture for either of ye to calm ye down, or anyways not many women or the wrong sort of women, and what's happened the bitterness has gone building up and building up without check, the daily grudges and faults and moans and baby-crimes against each other ye can never seem to step back from and see the love there underneath and forgive each other for. Now, what the point of me letter is, couldn't ye do something about it? Couldn't the both of ye, now, go stepping back and making a listeen of all the things about the other that do get on yere nerves, and the wrongs the other has done all down through the years that you still hold against him, and be reading them lists out, and be discussing them openly, and be taking a deep breath then and be forgiving each other them wrongs, no matter what they may be? Would that be so awful hard, now? It would for ye two, I know, but couldn't ye just be trying it, now? And if it doesn't work it doesn't work, but at least ye could say ye'd tried and would ye be any worse off? And if ye wouldn't be doing it for yourselves, wouldn't ye be doing it for me, now? For a friend of yeres, who cares about ye, who doesn't want to see ye blowing the brains out of each other, who never achieved anything as a priest in Leenane, in fact the opposite, and who'd see ye two becoming true brothers again as the greatest achievement of his whole time here. Sure it would be bordering on the miraculous. I might be canonised after. *(Pause.)* Valene and Coleman, I'm betting everything on ye. I know for sure there's love there somewheres, it's just a case of ye stepping back and looking for it. I'd be willing to bet me own soul that that love is there, and I know well the odds are stacked against me. They're probably 64,000 to one be this time, but I'd go betting on ye's still, for despite everything, despite yere murder and yere mayhem and yere miserliness that'd tear the teeth out of broken goats, I have faith in ye. You wouldn't be letting me down now, would ye? Yours sincerely and yours with the love of Christ now, Roderick Welsh. *(Pause. Welsh shivers slightly. Blackout.)*

Scene 3

Valene's house. Shotgun back on wall, over shelf full of new ceramic figurines, all marked with a 'V'. Coleman, in glasses, sits in the armchair left, glass of poteen beside him, perusing another women's magazine. Valene enters carrying a bag and places his hand on the stove in a number of places. Irritated, Coleman tries to ignore him.

VALENE.   I'm checking. *(Pause.)* It's good to have a little check. *(Pause.) I* think it is, d'you know? *(Pause.)* Just a *little* check. D'you know what I mean, like? *(After a while more of this, Valene takes some new ceramic figurines out of his bag, which he arranges with the others on the shelf.)*

COLEMAN.   Ah for....

VALENE.   Eh?

COLEMAN.   Eh?

VALENE.   Now then, eh?

COLEMAN.   Uh-huh?

VALENE.   Eh? Nice, I think. Eh? What do *you* think, Coleman?

COLEMAN.   I think you can go feck yourself.

VALENE.   No, not feck meself at all, now. Or over to the left a biteen would they look better? Hmm, we'll put the new St. Martin over here, so it balances out with the other St. Martin over there, so's we have one darkie saint on either side, so it balances out symmetrical, like. *(Pause.)* I'm a great one for shelf arranging I am. It is a skill I did never know I had. *(Pause.)* Forty-six figurines now. I'm sure to be getting into heaven with this many figurines in me house. *(Valene finds his pen and marks up the new figurines.)*

COLEMAN.   *(Pause.)* There's a poor girl born in Norway here with no lips.

VALENE.   *(Pause.)* That's old news that lip girl is.

COLEMAN.   That girl'll never be getting kissed. Not with the bare gums on her flapping.

VALENE. She's the exact same as you, so, if she'll never be getting kissed, and you've no excuse. You've the full complement of lips.

COLEMAN. I suppose a million girls you've kissed in your time. Oh aye.

VALENE. Nearer two million.

COLEMAN. Two million, aye. And all of them aunties when you was twelve.

VALENE. Not aunties at all. Proper women.

COLEMAN. Me brother Valentine does be living in his own little dream-world, with the sparrows and the fairies and the hairy little men. Puw-ooh! And the daisy people.

VALENE. *(Pause.)* I hope that's not my poteen.

COLEMAN. It's not at all your poteen.

VALENE. Uh-huh? *(Pause.)* Did you hear the news?

COLEMAN. I did. Isn't it awful?

VALENE. It's a disgrace. It's an outright disgrace, and nothing but. You can't go sending off an entire girl's football team, sure.

COLEMAN. Not in a semi-fecking-final anyways.

VALENE. Not at any time, sure. If you have to send people off you send them off one at a time, for their individual offences. You don't go slinging the lot of them off wholesale, and only seven minutes in, so they go crying home to their mammys.

COLEMAN. St. Josephine's have only got through be default, and nothing but default. If they had any honour they'd not take their place in the final at all and be giving it to us.

VALENE. I hope they lose the final.

COLEMAN. The same as that, *I* hope they lose the final. Sure, with their goalie in a coma they're bound to.

VALENE. No, their goalie came out of her coma a while ago there. Intensive care is all she's in now.

COLEMAN. She was fecking feigning? Getting us expelled from all competitions for no reason at all? I hope she relapses into her coma and dies.

VALENE. The same as that, *I* hope she lapses into her coma and dies. *(Pause.)* Look at us, we're in agreement.

COLEMAN. We are, I suppose.

VALENE. We can agree sometimes. *(Pause. He snatches the*

40

magazine out of Coleman's hands.) Except don't go reading me magazines, I've told you, 'til I've finished reading them. *(He sits at the table and flips through the magazine without reading it. Coleman fumes.)*

COLEMAN. *(Standing.)* And don't go ... don't go tearing them out of me fecking hands, near tore the fingers off me!

VALENE. Have these fingers you *(V-sign)* and take them to bed with ya.

COLEMAN. You're not even reading that *Take a Break.*

VALENE. I *am* reading this *Take a Break,* or anyways I'm glancing through this *Take a Break* at me own pace, as a fella's free to do if it's with his own money he goes buying his *Take a Break.*

COLEMAN. Only women's magazines is all you ever go reading. Sure without doubt it's a fecking gayboy you must be.

VALENE. There's a lad here in Bosnia and not only has he no arms but his mammy's just died. *(Mumbles as he reads, then:)* Ah they're only after fecking money, the same as ever.

COLEMAN. And no fear of you sending that poor no-armed boy any money, ah no.

VALENE. They've probably only got him to put his arms behind his back, just to cod ya.

COLEMAN. It's any excuse for you.

VALENE. And I bet his mammy's fine.

COLEMAN. *(Pause.)* Get *Bella* if you're getting magazines. *Take a Break's* nothing but quizzes.

VALENE. There's a coupon here for Honey Nut Loops. *(Valene starts carefully tearing out the coupon at the same time as Coleman quietly takes some Taytos out of a cupboard.)*

COLEMAN. Quizzes and deformed orphans. *(Pause.)* Em, would you let me be having a bag of Taytos, Val? I'm hungry a biteen.

VALENE. *(Looking up. Pause.)* Are you being serious, now?

COLEMAN. G'wan. I'll owe you for them.

VALENE. Put that bag back, now.

COLEMAN. I'll owe you for them, I'm saying. You can put them on the same bill you've put your melted figurines.

VALENE. Put them ... put them.... What are you doing, now?

Put them Taytos back, I said.

COLEMAN.   Valene, listen to me....

VALENE.   No....

COLEMAN.   I'm hungry and I need some Taytos. Didn't I wait 'til you came back in to ask you, now, and only because I'm honest....

VALENE.   And you've asked me and I've said no. Slinging insults at me Taytos the other week I remember is all you were. I see the boot's on the other foot now.

COLEMAN.   I've asked polite, now, Valene, and feck boots. Three times I've asked polite.

VALENE.   I know well you've asked polite, Coleman. You've asked awful polite. And what I'm saying to ya, ya can't have any of me fecking Taytos, now!

COLEMAN.   Is that your final word on the subject?

VALENE.   It *is* me final word on the subject.

COLEMAN.   *(Pause.)* I won't have any of your Taytos so. *(Pause.)* I'll just crush them to skitter. *(He crushes the crisps to pulp and tosses the packet at Valene. Valene darts up and around the table to get at Coleman, during which time Coleman grabs two more packets from the cupboard and holds them up, one in each hand, threatening to crush them also.)* Back off! *(Valene stops dead in his tracks.)* Back off or they'll be getting it the same!

VALENE.   *(Scared.)* Be leaving me crisps now, Coleman.

COLEMAN.   Be leaving them, is it? When all I wanted was to go buying one of them and would've paid the full whack, but oh no.

VALENE.   *(Tearfully, choking.)* That's a waste of good food that is, Coleman.

COLEMAN.   Good food, is it?

VALENE.   There's Bosnians'd be happy to have them Taytos. *(Coleman opens one of the bags and starts eating just as the front door bangs open and Girleen enters, face blotchy, letter in hand.)*

COLEMAN.   They *are* good food, d'you know?

GIRLEEN.   *(In shock throughout.)* Have you heard the news, now?

COLEMAN.   What news, Girleen? The under-twelves...? *(Seeing*

42

Coleman distracted, Valene dives for his neck, trying to get the crisps off him at the same time. They drag each other to the floor, rolling and scuffling, Coleman purposely mashing up the crisps any chance he gets. Girleen stares at them a while, then quietly takes a butcher's knife out of one of the drawers, goes over to them, pulls Coleman's head back by the hair and puts the knife to his neck.)

VALENE.   Leave Coleman alone, Girleen. What are you doing, now?

GIRLEEN.   I'm breaking ye up.

COLEMAN.   *(Scared.)* We're broke up.

VALENE.   *(Scared.)* We're broke up. *(Once the two are separated, Girleen lets Coleman go and puts the letter on the table, sadly.)*

GIRLEEN.   There's a letter there Father Welsh wrote ye.

VALENE.   What does that feck want writing to us?

COLEMAN.   Going moaning again, I'll bet. *(Valene picks the letter up, Coleman pulls it off him, Valene pulls it back. They stand reading it together, Coleman getting bored after a few seconds. Girleen takes out a heart pendant on a chain and looks at it.)*

GIRLEEN.   I read it already on ye, coming over. All about the two of ye loving each other as brothers it is.

COLEMAN.   *(Stifling laughter.)* Wha?

VALENE.   Father Walsh Welsh's leaving, it looks like.

COLEMAN.   Is it full of moaning, Valene? It is.

VALENE.   And nothing but moaning. *(Mimicking.)* 'Getting your hairstyle insulted is no just cause to go murdering someone, in fact it's the worst cause I did ever hear.'

COLEMAN.   *(Laughing.)* That was a funny voice.

GIRLEEN.   I did order him this heart on a chain out of me mam's Freeman's catalogue. Only this morning it came. I asked him to be writing me with his new address last night, so I could send it on to him. I'd've never've got up the courage to be giving it him to his face. I'd've blushed the heart out of me. Four months I've been saving up to buy it him. All me poteen money. *(Crying.)* All me poteen money gone. I should've skittered it away the boys in Carraroe, and not go pinning me hopes on a feck I knew full well I'd never have. *(Girleen cuts the chain in two with a knife.)*

43

COLEMAN. Don't be cutting your good chain there, Girleen.

VALENE. Be leaving your chaineen there now, Girleen. That chain looks worth something. *(Girleen tosses the chain in a corner.)*

GIRLEEN. *(Sniffling.)* Have you read the letter there, now?

VALENE. I have. A pile of oul bull.

GIRLEEN. I read it to see if he mentioned me. Not a word.

COLEMAN. Just shite is it, Valene? It's not worth reading?

VALENE. Not at all.

COLEMAN. I'll leave it so, for I've no time for letters. I've never seen the sense in them. They're just writing.

GIRLEEN. I did like the bit about him betting his soul on ye. Didn't ye like that bit? *(Valene picks up the broken chain.)*

VALENE. I don't think I understood that bit.

GIRLEEN. *(Pause.)* Father Welsh drowned himself in the lake last night, same place as Tom Hanlon. They dragged his body out this morning. His soul in hell he's talking about, that only ye can save for him. *(Pause.)* You notice he never asked me to go saving his soul. I'd've liked to've saved his soul. I'd've been honoured, but no. *(Crying.)* Only mad drunken pig-shite feck-brained thicks he goes asking. *(Shocked, Coleman reads the letter. Girleen goes to the door. Valene offers the pendant out to her.)*

VALENE. Your heart, Girleen, be keeping it for yourself.

GIRLEEN. *(Crying.)* Feck me heart. Feck it to hell. Toss it into fecking skitter's the best place for that fecking heart. *(Exiting.)* Not even a word to me! *(After Girleen exits, Valene sits in an armchair, looking at the chain. Coleman finishes reading the letter, leaves it on the table and sits in the opposite armchair.)*

VALENE. Did you read it?

COLEMAN. I did.

VALENE. *(Pause.)* Isn't it sad about him?

COLEMAN. It *is* sad. Very sad.

VALENE. *(Pause.)* Will we be trying for ourselves? To get along, now?

COLEMAN. We will.

VALENE. There's no harm in trying.

COLEMAN. No harm at all, sure.

VALENE. *(Pause.)* Poor Father Welsh Walsh Welsh.

COLEMAN. Welsh.

VALENE. Welsh. *(Pause.)* I wonder why he did it?

COLEMAN. I suppose he must've been upset o'er something.

VALENE. I suppose. *(Pause.)* This is a pricey chain. *(Pause.)* We'll be giving it back to her next time we see her. She's only shocked now.

COLEMAN. Aye. She's not in her right mind at all. She did hurt me hair when she tugged at it too, d'you know?

VALENE. It did look like it hurt.

COLEMAN. It did hurt.

VALENE. *(Pause.)* Father Welsh going topping himself does put arging o'er Taytos into perspective anyways.

COLEMAN. It does.

VALENE. Eh?

COLEMAN. It does.

VALENE. Aye. Awful perspective. Awful perspective.

COLEMAN. *(Pause.)* Did you see 'Roderick' his name is?

VALENE. *(Snorts.)* I did.

COLEMAN. *(Pause. Seriously.)* We shouldn't laugh. *(Valene nods. Both pull serious faces. Blackout.)*

Scene 4

Room tidier. Welsh's letter pinned to the foot of the crucifix. Valene and Coleman enter dressed in black, having just attended Welsh's funeral, Coleman carrying a small plastic bag full of sausage rolls and vol-au-vents. He sits at the table. Valene opens his poteen biscuit tin.

VALENE. That's that, then.

COLEMAN. That's that, aye. That's Father Welsh gone.

VALENE. A good do.

COLEMAN. Aye. It's often a good do when it's a priest they're sticking away. *(Coleman empties his bag onto table.)*

VALENE. You didn't have to go nabbing a whole bagful now, Coleman.

COLEMAN. Didn't they offer, sure?

VALENE. But a whole bagful, I'm saying.

COLEMAN. It'd have only gone to waste, and sure a bagful won't be going very far between us.

VALENE. Between us?

COLEMAN. Of course between us.

VALENE. Ohh. *(They both eat a little.)* These are nice vol-au-vents.

COLEMAN. They *are* nice vol-au-vents.

VALENE. You can't say the Catholic Church doesn't know how to make a nice vol-au-vent, now.

COLEMAN. It's their best feature. And their sausage rolls aren't bad either, although they probably only buy them in.

VALENE. *(Pause.)* Em, would you be having a glass of poteen with me, Coleman?

COLEMAN. *(Shocked.)* I would, now. If you can spare a drop, like.

VALENE. I can easy spare a drop. *(Valene pours two glasses, one bigger than the other, thinks about it, then gives Coleman the bigger.)*

COLEMAN. Thank you, Valene. Sure we have our own little feasteen now.

VALENE. We do.

COLEMAN. D'you remember when as gasurs we did used to put the blankets o'er the gap between our beds and hide under them like a tent it was o'er us, and go having a feasteen of oul jammy sandwiches then?

VALENE. That was you and Mick Dowd used to go camping in the gap between our beds. You'd never let me be in with yous at all. Ye used to step on me head if I tried to climb into that camp with you. I still remember it.

COLEMAN. Mick Dowd, was it? I don't remember that at all, now. I did think it was you.

VALENE. Half me childhood you spent stepping on me head, and for no reason. And d'you remember when you pinned me down and sat across me on me birthday and let the stringy spit dribble out your gob and let down and down it dribble 'til it landed in me eye then?

COLEMAN. I remember it well, Valene, and I'll tell you this. I did mean to suck that spit back up just before it got to your eye, but what happened I lost control o'er it.

VALENE. And on me birthday.

COLEMAN. (Pause.) I do apologise for dribbling in your eye and I do apologise for stepping on your head, Valene. On Father Welsh's soul I apologise.

VALENE. I do accept your apology so.

COLEMAN. Although plenty of times as a gasur I remember you dropping stones on me head while I was asleep and big stones.

VALENE. Only in retaliation them stones ever was.

COLEMAN. Retaliation or not. Waking up to stones dropping on ya is awful frightening for a small child. And retaliation doesn't count anyways if it's a week later. It's only then and there retaliation does apply.

VALENE. I do apologise for dropping stones on you so. (Pause.) For your brain never did recover from them injuries, did it, Coleman? (Coleman stares at Valene a second, then smiles. Valene smiles also.) This is a great oul game, this is, apologising. Father Welsh wasn't too far wrong.

COLEMAN. I hope Father Welsh isn't in hell at all. I hope he's in heaven.

VALENE. I hope he's in heaven.

COLEMAN. Or purgatory at worst.

VALENE. Although if he's in hell at least he'll have Tom Hanlon to speak to.

COLEMAN. So it won't be as if he doesn't know anybody.

VALENE. Aye. And the fella off Alias Smith and Jones.

COLEMAN. Is the fella off Alias Smith and Jones in hell?

VALENE. He is. Father Welsh was telling me.

COLEMAN. The blond one.

VALENE. No, the other one.

COLEMAN. He was good, the other one.

VALENE. He was the best one.

COLEMAN. It's always the best ones go to hell. Me, probably straight to heaven I'll go, even though I blew the head off poor dad. So long as I go confessing to it anyways. That's the good thing about being Catholic. You can shoot your dad in the head and it doesn't even matter at all.

VALENE. Well it matters a little bit.

COLEMAN. It matters a little bit but not a big bit.

VALENE. *(Pause.)* Did you see Girleen crying her eyes out, the funeral?

COLEMAN. I did.

VALENE. Poor Girleen. And her mam two times has had to drag her screaming from the lake at night, did you hear, there where Father Walsh jumped, and her just standing there, staring.

COLEMAN. She must've liked Father Welsh or something.

VALENE. I suppose she must've. *(Taking out Girleen's chain.)* She wouldn't take her chaineen back at all. She wouldn't hear tell of it. I'll put it up here with his letter to us. *(He attaches the chain to the cross, so the heart rests on the letter, which he gently smoothes out.)* It's the mental they'll be putting Girleen in before long if she carries on.

COLEMAN. Sure it's only a matter of time.

VALENE. Isn't that sad?

COLEMAN. Awful sad. *(Pause. Shrugging.)* Ah well. *(He eats another vol-au-vent. Valene remembers something, fishes in the pockets of his jacket, takes out two ceramic figurines, places them on the shelf, uncaps his pen almost automatically, thinks better of marking them as before, and puts the pen away.)* I think I'm getting to like vol-au-vents now. I think I'm developing a taste for them. We ought to go to more funerals.

VALENE. They do have them at weddings too.

COLEMAN. Do they? Who'll next be getting married round here so? Girleen I would used to have said, as pretty as she is, only she'll probably have topped herself before ever she gets married.

VALENE. *Me* probably'll be the next one getting married, as handsome as I am. Did you see today all the young nuns eyeing me?

COLEMAN. Who'd go marrying you, sure? Even that no-lipped girl in Norway'd turn you down.

VALENE. *(Pause. Angrily.)* See, I'm stepping back now ... I'm stepping back, like Father Walsh said and I'm forgiving ya, insulting me.

COLEMAN. *(Sincerely.)* Oh ... oh, I'm sorry now, Valene. I'm sorry. It just slipped out on me without thinking.

VALENE. No harm done so, if only an accident it was.

COLEMAN. It *was* an accident. Although remember you did insult me there earlier, saying I was brain-damaged be stones as a gasur, and I didn't even pull you up on it.

VALENE. I apologise for saying you was brain-damaged as a gasur so.

COLEMAN. No apology was necessary, Valene, and I have saved you the last vol-au-venteen on top of it.

VALENE. You have the last vol-au-vent, Coleman. I'm not overly keen on vol-au-vents. *(Coleman nods in thanks and eats the vol-au-vent.)* Weren't them young nuns lovely today now, Coleman.

COLEMAN. They was lovely nuns.

VALENE. They must've known Father Welsh from nun college or something.

COLEMAN. I'd like to touch them nuns both upstairs and downstairs, so I would. Except for the fat one on the end.

VALENE. She was a horror and she knew.

COLEMAN. If dad was there today he'd've just gone screaming at them nuns.

VALENE. Why *did* dad used to go screaming at nuns, Coleman?

COLEMAN. I don't have an idea at all why he used to scream at nuns. He must've had a bad experience with nuns as a child.

VALENE. If you hadn't blown the brains out of dad we could ask him outright. *(Coleman stares at him sternly.)* No, I'm not saying anything, now. I'm calm, I've stepped back, and I'm saying this quietly and without any spite at all, but you know well that that wasn't right, Coleman, shooting dad in the head on us. In your heart anyways you know.

COLEMAN. *(Pause.)* I *do* know it wasn't right. Not only in me heart but in me head and in me everywhere. I was wrong for shooting dad. I was dead wrong. And I'm sorry for it.

VALENE. And I'm sorry for sitting you down and making you sign your life away, Coleman. It was the only way at the time I could think of punishing ya. Well, I could've let you go to jail but I didn't want you going to jail and it wasn't out of miserliness that I stopped you going to jail. It was more out of I didn't want all on me own to be left here. I'd've missed ya. *(Pause.)* From this day on ... from this day on, this house and everything in this house is half yours again, Coleman. *(Touched, Coleman offers his hand out and they shake, embarrassed. Pause.)* Is there any other confessions we have to get off our chests, now we're at it?

COLEMAN. There must be millions. *(Pause.)* Crushing your crisps to skitter, Valene, I'm sorry for.

VALENE. I forgive you for it. *(Pause.)* Do you remember that holiday in Lettermullen as gasurs we had, and you left your cowboy stagecoach out in the rain that night and next morning it was gone and mam and dad said 'Oh it must've been hijacked be Indians.' It wasn't hijacked be Indians. I'd got up early and pegged it in the sea.

COLEMAN. *(Pause.)* I did love that cowboy stagecoach.

VALENE. I know you did, and I'm sorry for it.

COLEMAN. *(Pause.)* That string of gob I dribbled on you on your birthday. I didn't try to suck it up at all. I wanted it to hit your eye and I was glad. *(Pause.)* And I'm sorry for it.

VALENE. Okay. *(Pause.)* Maureen Folan did once ask me to ask you if you wanted to see a film at the Claddagh Palace with her, and she'd've driven ye and paid for dinner too, and from the tone of her voice it sounded like you'd've been on a promise after, but I never passed the message onto ya, out of nothing but pure spite.

COLEMAN. Sure that's no great loss, Valene. Maureen Folan looks like a thin-lipped ghost, with the hairstyle of a frightened red ape.

VALENE. But on a promise you'd've been.

COLEMAN. On a promise or no. That was nothing at all to go confessing. Okay, it's my go. I'm winning.

VALENE. What d'you mean, you're winning?

COLEMAN. *(Thinking.)* Do you remember your Ker-Plunk game?

VALENE.   I *do* remember me Ker-Plunk game.

COLEMAN.   It wasn't Liam Hanlon stole all them marbles out of your Ker-Plunk game at all, it was me.

VALENE.   What did you want me Ker-Plunk marbles for?

COLEMAN.   I went slinging them at the swans in Galway. I had a great time.

VALENE.   That ruined me Ker-Plunk. You can't play Ker-Plunk without marbles. And, sure, that was *both* of ours Ker-Plunk. That was just cutting off your nose to spite your face, Coleman.

COLEMAN.   I know it was and I'm sorry, Valene. Your go now. *(Pause.)* You're too slow. D'you remember when we had them backward children staying for B&B, and they threw half your *Spiderman* comics in on the fire? They didn't. D'you know who did? I did. I only blamed them cos they were too daft to arg.

VALENE.   They was good *Spiderman* comics, Coleman. Spiderman went fighting Doctor Octopus in them comics.

COLEMAN.   I'm sorry for it. Your go. *(Pause.)* You're too slow....

VALENE.   Hey...!

COLEMAN.   D'you remember when Pato Dooley beat the skitter out of you when he was twelve and you was twenty, and you never knew the reason why? I knew the reason why. I did tell him you'd called his dead mammy a hairy whore.

VALENE.   With a fecking chisel that Pato Dooley beat me up that day! Almost had me fecking eye out!

COLEMAN.   I think Pato must've liked his mammy or something. *(Pause.)* I'm awful sorry for it, Valene. *(Coleman burps lazily.)*

VALENE.   You do sound it!

COLEMAN.   Shall I be having another go?

VALENE.   I did pour a cup of piss in a pint of lager you drank one time, Coleman. Aye, and d'you know what, now? You couldn't even tell the differ.

COLEMAN.   *(Pause.)* When was this, now?

VALENE.   When you was seventeen, this was. D'you remember that month you were laid up in hospital with bacterial tonsilitis. Around then it was. *(Pause.)* And I'm sorry for it, Coleman.

COLEMAN.   I do take your poteen out its box each week, drink the half of it and fill the rest back up with water. Ten years this has been going on. You haven't tasted full-strength poteen since nineteen eighty-fecking-three.

VALENE. *(Drinks. Pause.)* But you're sorry for it.

COLEMAN. I suppose I'm sorry for it, aye. *(Mumbling.)* Making me go drinking piss, and not just anybody's piss but *your* fecking piss....

VALENE. *(Angrily.)* But you're sorry for it, you're saying?!

COLEMAN. I'm sorry for it, aye! I'm fecking sorry for it! Haven't I said?!

VALENE. That's okay, so, if you're sorry for it, although you don't sound fecking sorry for it.

COLEMAN. You can kiss me fecking arse so, Valene, if you don't ... I'm taking a step back now, so I am. *(Pause.)* I'm sorry for watering your poteen down all these years, Valene. I am, now.

VALENE. Good-oh. *(Pause.)* Is it your go now or is it mine?

COLEMAN. I think it might be your go, Valene.

VALENE. Thank you, Coleman. D'you remember when Alison O'Hoolihan went sucking that pencil in the playground that time, and ye were to go dancing the next day, but somebody nudged that pencil and it got stuck in her tonsils on her, and be the time she got out of hospital she was engaged to the doctor who wrenched it out for her and wouldn't be giving you a fecking sniffeen. Do you remember, now?

COLEMAN. I do remember.

VALENE. That was me nudged that pencil, and it wasn't an accident at all. Pure jealous I was. *(Pause. Coleman throws his sausage rolls in Valene's face and dives over the table for his neck. Valene dodges the attack.)* And I'm sorry for it! I'm sorry for it! *(Pointing at letter.)* Father Welsh! Father Welsh! *(Valene fends Coleman off. They stand staring at each other, Coleman seething.)*

COLEMAN. Eh?!!

VALENE. Eh?

COLEMAN. I did fecking love Alison O'Hoolihan! We may've been married today if it hadn't been for that fecking pencil!

VALENE. What was she doing sucking it the pointy end inwards anyways? She was looking for trouble!

COLEMAN. And she fecking found it with you! That pencil

52

could've killed Alison O'Hoolihan!

VALENE. And I'm sorry for it, I said. What are you doing pegging good sausage rolls at me? Them sausage rolls cost money. You were suppose to have taken a step back and went calming yourself, but you didn't, you just flew off the handle. Father Welsh's soul'll be roasting now because of you.

COLEMAN. Leave Father Welsh's soul out of it. This is about you sticking pencils down poor girl's gobs on them.

VALENE. That pencil is water under a bridge and I've apologised whole-hearted for that pencil. *(Sits down.)* And she had boss-eyes anyways.

COLEMAN. She didn't have boss-eyes! She had nice eyes!

VALENE. Well there was something funny about them.

COLEMAN. She had nice brown eyes.

VALENE. Oh aye. *(Pause.)* Well it's your go now, Coleman. Try and top that one for yourself. Heh.

COLEMAN. Try and top that one, is it?

VALENE. It is. *(Coleman thinks for a moment, smiles slightly, then sits back down.)*

COLEMAN. I've taken a step back now.

VALENE. I can see you've taken a step back.

COLEMAN. I'm pure calm now. It does be good to get things off your chest.

VALENE. It *does* be good. I'm glad that pencil-nudging's off me chest. I can sleep nights now.

COLEMAN. Is it a relief to ya?

VALENE. It *is* a relief to me. *(Pause.)* What have you got cooking up?

COLEMAN. I have one and I'm terrible sorry for it. Oh terrible sorry I am.

VALENE. I won't be near as good as me pencilling poor boss-eyed Alison, whatever it is.

COLEMAN. Ah I suppose your right, now. My one's only a weeny oul one. D'you remember you always thought it was Mairtin Hanlon snipped the ears off of poor Lassie, now?

VALENE. *(Confidently.)* I don't believe you at all. You're only making it up now, see.

COLEMAN. It wasn't wee Mairtin at all. D'you know who it was, now?

VALENE. Me arse was it you. You'll have to be doing better than that, now, Coleman.

COLEMAN. To the brookeen I dragged him, me scissors in hand, and him whimpering his fat gob off 'til the deed was done and he dropped down dead with not a fecking peep out of that whiny fecking dog.

VALENE. D'you see, it doesn't hurt me at all when you go making up lies. You don't understand the rules, Coleman. It does have to be true, else it's just plain daft. You can't go claiming credit for snipping the ears off a dog when you didn't lay a finger on that dog's ears, and the fecking world knows.

COLEMAN. *(Pause.)* Is it evidence, so, you're after?

VALENE. It *is* evidence I'm after, aye. Go bring me evidence you did cut the ears off me dog. And be quick with that evidence.

COLEMAN. I won't be quick at all. I will take me time. *(He slowly gets up and ambles to his room, closing its door behind him. Valene waits patiently, giving a worried laugh. After a ten-second pause, Coleman ambles back on, carrying a slightly wet brown paper bag. He pauses at the table a moment for dramatic effect, slowly opens the bag, pulls out a dog's big fluffy black ear, lays it on top of Valene's head, takes out the second ear, pauses, places that on Valene's head also, puts the empty bag down on the table, smoothes it out, then sits down in the armchair L. Valene has been staring out into space all the while, dumbstruck. He tilts his head so that the ears fall down onto the table, and he stares at them a while. Coleman picks up Valene's felt-tip pen, brings it over and lays it on the table.)* There's your little pen, now, Val. Why don't you mark them dog's ears with your V, so we'll be remembering who they belong to. *(He sits back down in the armchair.)* And do you want to hear something else, Valene? I'm sorry for cutting off them dog's ears. With all me fecking heart I'm sorry, oh aye, because I've tooken a step back now, look at me.... *(He half-laughs through his nose. Valene gets up, stares blankly at Coleman a moment, goes to the cupboard R. and, with his back to Coleman, pulls the butcher's knife out of it. In the same brief second Coleman stands,*

54

pulls the shotgun down from above the stove and sits down with it. Valene turns, knife ready. The gun is pointed directly at him. Valene wilts slightly, thinks about it a moment, regains his courage and his anger, and slowly approaches Coleman, raising the knife. Surprised, slightly scared.) What are you doing now, Valene?

VALENE. *(Blankly.)* Oh not a thing am I doing, Coleman, other than killing ya.

COLEMAN. Be putting that knife back in that drawer, you.

VALENE. No, I'll be putting it in the head of you, now.

COLEMAN. Don't you see me gun?

VALENE. Me poor fecking Lassie, who never hurt a flea. *(Valene has gotten all the way up to Coleman, so that the barrel of the gun is touching his chest. He raises the knife to its highest point.)*

COLEMAN. What are you doing, now? Stop it.

VALENE. I'll stop it, all right....

COLEMAN. Father Welsh's soul, Valene. Father Wel....

VALENE. Father Welsh's soul me fecking arse! Father Welsh's soul didn't come into play when you hacked me dog's ears off him and kept them in a bag!

COLEMAN. Ar that was a year ago. How does that apply?

VALENE. Be saying good-bye to the world, you, ya feck!

COLEMAN. *You'll* have to be saying good-bye to the world too, so, because I'll be bringing you with me.

VALENE. Do I look like I mind that at all, now?

COLEMAN. *(Pause.)* Er er, wait wait wait, now....

VALENE. Wha...?

COLEMAN. Look at me gun. Look at me gun where it's going, do ya see...? *(Coleman slides the gun away and down from Valene's chest 'til it points directly at the door of the stove.)*

VALENE. *(Pause.)* Be pointing that gun away from me stove, now.

COLEMAN. I won't be. Stab away, now. It's your stove it'll be'll be going with me instead of ya.

VALENE. Leave ... what...? That was a three-hundred-pound stove now, Coleman....

COLEMAN. I know well it was.

VALENE. Be leaving it alone. That's just being sly, that is.

COLEMAN. Be backing off you with that knife, you sissy-arse.

VALENE. *(Tearfully.)* You're not a man at all, pointing guns at stoves.

COLEMAN. I don't care if I am or I'm not. Be backing off, I said.

VALENE. You're just a ... you're just a....

COLEMAN. Eh?

VALENE. Eh?

COLEMAN. Eh?

VALENE. You're not a man at all, you.

COLEMAN. Be backing away now, you, cry-baby. Be taking a step back for yourself. Eheh.

VALENE. *(Pause.)* I'm backing away now, so I am.

COLEMAN. That'd be the best thing, aye. *(Valene slowly retreats, lays the knife on the table and sits down there sadly, gently stroking his dog's ears. Coleman is still pointing the gun at the stove door. He shakes his head slightly.)* I can't believe you raised a knife to me. No, I can't believe you raised a knife to your own brother.

VALENE. You raised a knife to me own dog and raised a gun to our own father, did a lot more damage than a fecking knife, now.

COLEMAN. No, I can't believe it. I can't believe you raised a knife to me.

VALENE. Stop going on about raising a knife, and be pointing that gun away from me fecking stove, now, in case it does go off be accident.

COLEMAN. Be accident, is it?

VALENE. Is the safety catch on that gun, now?

COLEMAN. The safety catch, is it?

VALENE. Aye, the safety catch! The safety catch! Is it ten million times I have to be repeating meself?

COLEMAN. The safety catch, uh-huh ... *(He jumps to his feet, points the gun down at the stove and fires, blowing the right-hand side apart. Valene falls to his knees in horror, his face in his hands. Coleman cocks the gun again and blows the left hand side apart also, then nonchalantly sits back down.)* No, the safety catch isn't on at all, Valene. Would you believe it? *(Pause. Valene is still kneeling there, dumbstruck.)* And I'll tell you another thing ... *(He suddenly jumps*

56

*up again and, holding the shotgun by the barrel, starts smashing it vio-
lently into the figurines, shattering them to pieces and sending them
flying around the room until not a single one remains standing. Valene
screams throughout. After Coleman has finished he sits again, the gun
across his lap. Valene is still kneeling. Pause.)* And don't go making
out that you didn't deserve it, because we both know full well
that you did.

VALENE. *(Numbly.)* You've broken all me figurines, Coleman.

COLEMAN. I have. Did you see me?

VALENE. And you've blown me stove to buggery.

COLEMAN. This is a great gun for blowing holes in things.

VALENE. *(Standing.)* And now you do have no bullets left in
that great gun. *(He lazily picks the knife back up and approaches
Coleman. But as he does so Coleman opens the barrel of the gun, tosses
away the spent cartridges, fishes in his pocket, comes out with a clenched
fist that may or may not contain another cartridge, shows the fist to
Valene and loads, or pretends to load, the bullet into the gun, without
Valene or the audience at any time knowing if there is a bullet or not.
Coleman snaps the barrel shut and lazily points it at Valene's head.)*
There was no bullet in that hand, Coleman! No bullet at all!

COLEMAN. Maybe there wasn't, now. Maybe it's pretending I
am. Be taking a pop for yourself.

VALENE. I *will* be taking a pop for meself.

COLEMAN. And then we'll see.

VALENE. *(Long, long pause.)* I want to kill you, Coleman.

COLEMAN. Ar, don't be saying that, now, Val.

VALENE. *(Sadly.)* It's true, Coleman. I want to kill you.

COLEMAN. *(Pause.)* Try so. *(Coleman cocks the gun. Pause. Valene
turns the knife around and around in his hand, staring at Coleman all
the while, until his head finally droops and he returns the knife to the
drawer. Coleman uncocks the gun, stands, and lays it down on the table,
staying near it. Valene idles to the stove and touches the letter pinned
above it.)*

VALENE. Father Welsh is burning in hell, now, because of our
fighting.

COLEMAN. Well did we ask him to go betting his soul on us?
No. And, sure, it's pure against the rules for priests to go betting
anyways, neverminding with them kinds of stakes. Sure a fiver

would've been overdoing it on us, let alone his soul. And what's wrong with fighting anyways? I do like a good fight. It does show you care, fighting does. That's what oul sissy Welsh doesn't understand. Don't you like a good fight?

VALENE.   I *do* like a good fight, the same as that. Although I don't like having me dog murdered on me, and me fecking dad murdered on me.

COLEMAN.   And I'm sorry for your dog and dad, Valene. I *am* sorry. Truly I'm sorry. And nothing to do with Father Welsh's letter is this at all. From me own heart this is. The same goes for your stove and your poor figurines too. Look at them. That was pure temper, that was. Although, admit it, you asked for that stove and them figurines.

VALENE.   You never fecking stop, you. *(Pause.) Are* you sorry, Coleman?

COLEMAN.   I am, Valene.

VALENE.   *(Pause.)* Maybe Father Walsh's Welsh's soul'll be all right so.

COLEMAN.   Maybe it will now. Maybe it will.

VALENE.   He wasn't such a bad fella.

COLEMAN.   He wasn't.

VALENE.   He wasn't a great fella, but he wasn't a bad fella.

COLEMAN.   Aye. *(Pause.)* He was a *middling* fella.

VALENE.   He was a *middling* fella.

COLEMAN.   *(Pause.)* I'm going out for a drink for meself. Will you be coming with me?

VALENE.   Aye, in a minute now I'll come. *(Coleman goes to the front door. Valene looks over the smashed figurines sadly.)*

COLEMAN.   I'll help you be clearing your figurines up when I get back, Valene. Maybe we can glue some of them together. Do you still have your Superglue?

VALENE.   I do have me Superglue, although I think the top's gone hard.

COLEMAN.   Aye, that's the trouble with Superglue.

VALENE.   Ah, the house insurance'll cover me figurines anyways. As well as me stove.

COLEMAN.   Oh....

VALENE.   *(Pause.)* What, 'oh?

COLEMAN.   Do you remember a couple of weeks ago there when you asked me did I go stealing your insurance money and I said no, I paid it in for you?

VALENE.   I do remember.

COLEMAN.   *(Pause.)* I didn't pay it in at all. I pocketed the lot of it, pissed it up a wall. *(Valene, seething, darts for the gun. Coleman dashes out through the front door. Valene brings the gun to the door and chases out, but Coleman is long gone. Valene returns a few seconds later, gun in hand, shaking with rage, almost in tears. After a while he begins to calm down, taking deep breaths. He looks down at the gun in his hands a moment, then gently opens the barrel to see if Coleman had really loaded it earlier. He had. Valene takes the cartridge out.)*

VALENE.   He'd've fecking shot me too. He'd've shot his own fecking brother! On top of his dad! On top of me stove! *(He tosses the gun and cartridge away, rips Father Welsh's letter off the cross, knocking Girleen's chain onto the floor, brings the letter back to the table and takes out a box of matches.)* And you, you whiny fecking priest. Do I need your soul hovering o'er me the rest of me fecking life? How could anybody be getting on with that feck? *(He strikes a match and lights the letter, which he glances over as he holds up. After a couple of seconds, the letter barely singed, Valene blows the flames out and looks at it on the table, sighing. Quietly.)* I'm too fecking kind-hearted is my fecking trouble. *(He returns to the cross and pins the chain and letter back onto it, smoothing the letter out. He puts on his jacket, checks it for loose change and goes to the front door.)* Well I won't be buying the fecker a pint anyways. I'll tell you that for nothing, Father Welsh Walsh Welsh. *(Valene glances back at the letter a second, sadly, looks down at the floor, then exits. Lights fade, with one light lingering on the crucifix and letter a half second longer than the others.)*

PROPERTY LIST

Biscuit tin with bottle of poteen (COLEMAN, VALENE)
Drinking glasses (COLEMAN, VALENE)
Carrier bag with fibreglass figurines (VALENE)
Felt tipped pen (VALENE)
Bag with 2 bottles of poteen (GIRLEEN)
Envelope with cheque (GIRLEEN)
Money (VALENE)
Glass of poteen (COLEMAN)
Woman's Own magazine
Reading glasses (COLEMAN)
Bag (VALENE) with:
    2 plastic figurines
    8 bags of Taytos
Insurance book (VALENE)
Coins (COLEMAN, VALENE)
Matches (COLEMAN, VALENE)
Large, oven-proof bowl (COLEMAN)
Plastic figurines (COLEMAN)
Comb (COLEMAN)
Towel (VALENE)
Bowl with half-melted figurines (VALENE)
Shotgun (VALENE, COLEMAN)
2 shotgun cartridges (COLEMAN)
Pint of Guinness (WELSH)
Letter (WELSH, GIRLEEN, VALENE)
Woman's magazine (COLEMAN)
Bag with ceramic figurines (VALENE)
Bag of Taytos (COLEMAN)
Butchers knife (GIRLEEN, VALENE)
Heart pendant (GIRLEEN)
Chain (GIRLEEN, VALENE)
Knife (GIRLEEN)
Bag full of sausage rolls and vol-au-vents (COLEMAN)
2 ceramic figurines (VALENE)
Wet, brown paper bag with 2 fluffy dog's ears (COLEMAN)
Gun cartridge (VALENE)

NOTES
(Use this space to make notes for your production)

NOTES

(Use this space to make notes for your production)